T0108145

# HOW TO
## TALK TO
# GIRLS

# HOW TO TALK TO GIRLS

Jonathan Toussaint

ALLEN&UNWIN

# CONTENTS

# ABOUT THE AUTHOR

Dr Jonathan Toussaint is a leading educator in the field of male health and an advocate for boys' education. He has been facilitating groups for men and boys for over 30 years, helping them address issues of gender, sexuality and communication. Jonathan practises as a counsellor and educator, and has developed leading-edge procedures that strengthen the family and community. He has a keen interest in working with men and boys, helping them discover more sensitive, respectful and personally rewarding ways of relating to others. Jonathan currently serves as a director of Interrelate Family Centres. He manages the company's sexuality education program in which more than 30 000 students and family members participate each year.

# ACKNOWLEDGEMENTS

Many people have contributed ideas and knowledge to this book. My thanks go to the countless students, colleagues, friends and educators for their willingness to share their personal stories with me informally, and in workshops and classrooms.

Special thanks to the young people who spoke with me and who I have quoted throughout this book. I have given them different names to protect their privacy. Their frankness and generosity have helped bring this book to life.

I am grateful to Maddy Phelan, Dianne Todaro, Janet and Jake Wilson and Elizabeth Morrison whose contributions and wisdom downloads have shaped my thinking and enriched this book. Also to all the staff at Allen & Unwin who believed in the book and the importance of the issues it raises.

I am indebted to my wife Karen and children Nathan and Sarah who are a constant source of inspiration, and who have taught me the importance of respectful relationships.

# INTRODUCTION

I remember when I was at school and girls were, well, maybe my friends—sometimes I talked to them but most of the time I just ignored them. They played and chatted with each other while I kicked a ball around with my mates. So why did it change? Why did girls I once ignored all of a sudden become so important to me? Why did I find it so hard to talk to them? Why did I want to impress them?

Welcome to the world of puberty, adolescence and being a teenager! When your body starts to change, your voice begins to deepen, spots appear, hair starts to grow on your face and body (and your mother becomes shorter than you!) that's when you began to notice GIRLS. Girls too go through similar changes: their bodies alter, they start to develop boobs, and they begin to have periods. More importantly, they begin to notice BOYS! They change and grow into attractive young women wanting boys to admire them. It is all part of growing up!

Over the years, I've spoken to thousands of boys and their

dads and what I've found is that different boys want different things from a relationship. Some want to be in love, some want a casual sexual relationship, some want romance, and others want someone to be close to. It takes time to find someone who wants the same as you.

Remember it's okay to take your time and ask yourself some questions: What do I want from a relationship? What don't I want? What qualities do I like in a person? What don't I like?

This book will give you an insight into what it is to be a boy. It will help you understand how boys talk and relate to each other (in comparison to those strange creatures called girls); how to get to know girls (what you should do and not do!); how to play the dating game; how to act at school dances, formals and socials and survive; how to try to make things better when everything goes wrong; and, lastly, this book gives some tips and hints about what it takes to have healthy relationships. It's a great time in your life—ENJOY IT!

# 1 SPEAKING UP FOR YOURSELF

All humans communicate no matter who they are. It's something people love to do. If you think about the reasons we talk to each other you'll come up with a list that includes getting information, telling each other stuff, seeking help, understanding each other, and having fun together. Good communication helps with everything you do each day—how would you get anything done with other people if you didn't talk? This exchange of ideas is a powerful tool, and the better you know how to do it the more you will enjoy talking to others and gaining benefit from it.

## BOYS ARE ALWAYS WANTING TO KNOW, 'HOW DO I GET A GIRL TO LIKE ME?' THE ANSWER IS (SO NOT) A BIG SECRET: BE A GOOD COMMUNICATOR!

Good communication can get you further than you think. It might help you to get a part-time job, to do better in school, to make close friends, and to talk to a girl. Boys are always wanting to know, 'How do I get a girl to like me?' The answer is (so not) a big secret: be a good communicator!

## What's stopping you?

A lot of people think that boys don't talk, which is so not true. Yes, some boys do seem to talk less than most girls, but don't let that fool you. Boys can communicate just as well as girls. But everyone finds talking to people hard sometimes, particularly when you are in a situation where you're not sure of what others expect of you. Your parents, friends and teachers all think you should act a certain way, and society's expectations are one of the things that make a huge impact on everyone's life. It might seem weird to think that 'society'—that big mass of traditions, laws and beliefs—actually can affect you as an individual. But think about it. Without doubt, years and years of people interacting in a certain way created particular values that shaped who you are.

Sometimes, though, these expectations become outdated or turn bad. Thankfully, ideas about masculinity have changed a lot and are improving all the time. People know that the

## MYTHS

» Boys don't cry.
» Boys don't talk much.
» Boys are tough.
» Real men don't express emotions.
» Boys like to fight.
» Boys should be macho.

old stereotype of boys being aggressive, testosterone-fuelled machines just doesn't cut it. Think about some of the things said about boys in the list above.

You know that these are just clichés and neither you nor your friends will feel inside that they are true. If all boys and men were like this they'd only be able to manage a caveman-like grunt! Stereotypes can actually be harmful because nobody fits a certain mould. Think about this list and the effect it can have on someone and then think about the kind of boy you are. Do you feel that the way others believe you should be is making it hard for you to communicate?

It's a good idea to also think about the rituals you have. Rituals are the things we regularly do in different situations. Families have rituals, like having pizza on Saturday night, and these often make you feel like part of the group. When you're hanging out with your mates you will have different rituals, like going surfing or playing soccer on Saturday afternoon. Maybe you jam with your mates and play the guitar in your garage band. So not all rituals are bad. But if you and your mates do things that lead to harmful behaviour through a sort of pack/group mentality, you could be making life a whole lot harder for yourself.

Humans are animals that like to be in social groups. But have you ever seen a tribe of monkeys go wild? Or a herd of wildebeest stampede? Groups of people can send signals to one another through words and gestures that lead the whole group to behaving in a certain way, and the unfortunate truth is that negative signals work best in a crowd. One person can spread fear or hate through a crowd just by sending the signals and waiting for people to catch on. Just think about how riots happen. Someone says something, a few people decide they will support them and become riled up, then a few more join in and it starts to get violent, and a lot of other people follow suit. Think about the mates you hang out with. Do you know of a group of boys whose behaviour got out of hand when a few guys decided to be violent or stupid? Ask yourself, do I really want to be a sheep that follows and doesn't think for itself? Learn to take a step back to make up your own mind about a situation before you become part of it.

You need to have a think about your own rituals, and the rituals that you and your mates are involved in. Some rituals can stop you from being yourself, or make you feel pressured to do things you don't want to do. This might actually block your ability to say what you think is right and stop you being a good communicator.

THERE'S THIS THING
CALLED THE 'BOY CODE'.

# EVERYONE HAS A DIFFERENT WAY OF EXPRESSING THEMSELVES.

## Busting boy myths

There's this thing called the 'boy code' (named by Dr William S. Pollack) and it sums up the bad rituals that exist in groups of boys. A lot of it comes down to hiding your emotions, acting tough and not communicating what you really think—the clichés we listed previously. A lot of men grew up with this 'boy code'—talk to your dad or a male teacher about it and you may be surprised by what they experienced and how it influenced them. You've probably seen the 'code' played out on TV shows—males just not being able to talk about their feelings—as it makes good television drama, but in real life it can be a problem if you believe that that's how you should be. A lot of difficulties men experience later on comes from the expectation that they are meant to be tough, not sensitive.

*Real men don't express emotion.* Don't start thinking this way, or that men can't feel! Men feel emotions just as much as women, but they suffer most when they can't talk about them. Depression, divorce and illness affect men but if they try to deal with these shattering emotions and events alone, without any support, then the harm can be long term. Society is changing and nowadays people are open to boys talking about what they think and how they feel. Even though this sometimes can lead to you being labelled a SNAG (sensitive, new-age guy), it is an important thing to think about. Going against the 'boy code' doesn't mean giving up your masculinity; you can still be a sweaty, energetic boy, but that's not the sum of you. You can also be a guy who talks about his feelings and beliefs, and be proud of them.

## THE 'BOY CODE' SAYS YOU'RE NOT ALLOWED TO FEEL ANY OF THE SISSY STUFF.

Let's tackle some of those myths listed earlier because, if you take them for granted, you might end up being labelled a non-feeling hardarse. The only way to prevent this is to understand what these myths are.

**Boys don't cry.** The 'boy code' says you're not allowed to feel any of the sissy stuff like love, compassion and sadness, or worse, to shed a lonely tear, let alone cry. That's just for chicks. But research shows that both boys and girls feel heaps of different emotions, and they need to be able to express these.

Otherwise it all gets bottled up (and might explode at any time!). Think about the last time your feelings were hurt—did you show it? There's the unwritten law (the 'boy code') that says boys don't cry. But anyone with a brain in his head can see that this is a lie. When a situation arises and you really do feel emotional about it, don't be ashamed to let it out—your mates might even respect you more for it as they *will* know what it feels like. Heaps of boys are in the same position as you: when it hurts, it hurts bad. Be brave and show your feelings, and you might just be opening up a new way of being for your mates as they will realise it is safe in your company to express emotions.

*Boys don't talk much.* Everyone has a different way of expressing themselves. Some people like to talk lots, some a little; others pepper their conversations with 'ums' and 'ahs' while they think, some just blurt things out. But maybe you don't see the point of talking much—I mean, talking isn't going to change anything, right? But if you've never tried to talk it out, you'll never know how much it can help. By opening up to people, you give them the chance to open up to you too. Don't let the 'boy code' be your guide here.

THERE'S THE UNWRITTEN LAW (THE 'BOY CODE') THAT SAYS BOYS DON'T CRY. BUT ANYONE WITH A BRAIN IN HIS HEAD CAN SEE THAT THIS IS A LIE.

CAVEMAN GRUNTING MIGHT BE WHAT THE 'BOY CODE' EXPECTS OF YOU, BUT HOW BORING IS THAT?

You are entitled to talk about whatever you wish and about what you like, whether the conversation is about your feelings or what you did on the weekend. Don't sell yourself short—caveman grunting might be what the 'boy code' expects of you, but how boring is that? Think about the conversations you have with your mates. A healthy group of friends allows each member to discuss whatever is on his mind. Are the rituals between your mates preventing you from talking as much as you'd like?

Boys who can talk about stuff generally find it easier to deal with difficult things. If something bad happened to you, such as the dog you've had since you were a kid dies, would you be able to talk about it with your mates? Good mates chat, just like girls do (well, maybe about different things). You might even discover that a friend of yours lost his dog a few years ago and he may be able to tell you what he did to cope and feel better. If the 'boy code' is so embedded in your thinking, you might find it hard to break out initially. But, when you do, it may open your world and nurture closer friendships with your mates.

***Boys are tough; they like to fight and should be macho.*** You might remember the Cronulla riots a while back. Someone sent

# PLAYING THE MACHO GUY IS NOT MUCH FUN.

a text message and what followed was a whole bunch of guys going down to the beach to protest but ending up rioting in the streets for hours. This is a prime example of the 'boy code'—the type of male that boys are expected to be: tough, macho, violent people, full of testosterone and aggression. 'Boys will be boys', so to speak, and if that means boys sometimes get into fights, well that's just how it is. But playing the macho guy is not much fun. Dangerous rituals like drinking excessive amounts of alcohol or getting into fights make it harder to build real trust with others, including your mates. You end up hiding behind the image.

Trust is the key ingredient to help you and your mates fight the 'boy code'. If you need to burn up energy, would you be better off getting into a fight or playing a clean game of touch rugby? You can burn off some energy with positive rituals. You also need to feel safe in your group, and not feel pressured to be violent and destructive. Negative rituals don't help anyone. It's a fact that innocent boys have died after being attacked by gangs of other boys. This is proof that if you allow the 'boy code' to drive you to violence, something is wrong. You only end up hurting yourself. Don't be a sucker—real men know how to keep the peace.

## JUST BECAUSE EVERYONE'S DOING IT, IT DOESN'T MEAN IT'S COOL.

Know when to walk away. This might mean leaving your group for a while, but it would be worth it. Sometimes you have to decide when to exit a situation. If your mates are being violent, playing dangerous games or doing illegal stuff, you need to consider whether you want to be a part of it or not. Just because everyone's doing it, it doesn't mean it's cool. And it doesn't mean you have to do it too! It's easy to just go with the flow but remember everyone in the group is responsible for the outcome of any actions done. Maybe you personally won't throw the first stone but, if you participated or stood by and let it develop, you're still a part of what happened. Be confident enough to be your own person and speak up.

Think about the consequences. It's all fun and games until someone loses an eye, right? Perhaps you don't realise it, but what you and your mates do might have serious consequences. Graffitiing might be fun, but there are serious penalties, such as fines and gaol time. Setting things on fire could be a cool backyard experiment, but what if it gets out of control? Just step back and think logically about what bad things could result from what you and your mates are getting up to, and then decide whether you want to keep going.

Real men know when to say 'no'. It's pretty tough trying to stand up to your mates. If you know that what your friends are doing is wrong, you need to have the guts to tell them to stop. Maybe they're teasing a girl you know, or stealing stuff, but if you think it's a bad idea, don't just walk away—say something. If you don't tell your mates that this is a bad idea then you may as well be saying, 'Yes, let's do it'. Sometimes your mates need a friend to tell them what they're doing is wrong. Be the responsible one and turn the crowd in the right direction.

## More than just talking

You can talk about heaps of stuff with your mates—music, girls, TV—but what is real talking? That's when you sit down and discuss the big issues with someone. Just talking is good, but real communication involves sharing. You can choose who you want to share with, who you trust—your best mate, your dad, your brother or your coach, whoever makes you feel comfortable and won't go telling other people what you've said. More than just talking is when you show how you feel or what you're really thinking about. It's when you have a problem and you talk to someone about it. It's when you go to someone else and tell

SPEAKING UP FOR YOURSELF

**29**

JUST TALKING IS GOOD, BUT REAL
COMMUNICATION INVOLVES SHARING.

them what's on your mind. And hopefully, it's when the other person can help you.

Maybe one of your mates will come up to you one day to do more than just talk about everyday stuff. Maybe he wants to ask out a girl, but doesn't know how. Maybe it's something more serious, like a family problem. When that happens, you need to be the trustworthy one. That means sharing in return, and by doing so you're offering to help them as much as you can. You'd expect the same if you went to someone else for support.

Be open and observant. Try to make sure you don't miss the signs when someone wants to really communicate with you. Sometimes people try to hide their real problems by turning it into a laugh, making jokes about it. Try to help them by recognising the cues so that you know when someone wants to really talk, and when you need to communicate with them in turn. Talking about an issue or feeling, really talking, with someone else can solve a lot of problems.

TALKING ABOUT AN ISSUE OR FEELING
CAN SOLVE A LOT OF PROBLEMS

# 2 BOY TALK

Maddison (15) said to me, 'Sometimes girls have really close guy friends who they can open up to. And that's how boys learn to talk to girls.' But what do you talk about when you talk to girls? The things you feel comfortable talking about with your mates are pretty different to what you might feel you can talk about with girls, or even what you think girls talk about with their friends. Think about what you chat about with your friends and then ask yourself whether you can talk about most of these topics with girls as well. Also consider what subjects you wouldn't discuss with a girl. It's good to get these two issues—what you can and what you can't talk to a girl about—clear in your mind so you're prepared. Which means next time you're talking to a girl you will be able to say to yourself, 'It's cool—I know what things I can say to her.'

'SOMETIMES GIRLS HAVE REALLY CLOSE GUY FRIENDS WHO THEY CAN OPEN UP TO. AND THAT'S HOW BOYS LEARN TO TALK TO GIRLS.'

## What interests you?

There are all sorts of things boys talk about with each other, depending on what you're interested in. The following is a list of stuff you might chat about with your mates, and there are probably a million other different topics you could discuss, depending on what you have in common:

This is not a list of everything; it's just to get you thinking about what you and your friends talk about. Write down all the things that interest you and your mates. In the list alongside, you could talk to a girl about pretty much everything, except maybe 'girls you think are hot'—then again, you may have female friends who are cool hearing about that kind of thing but you will have to return the favour and hear what guys she thinks are hot!

There are also some things that girls might not like as much as boys do, like cars or sport, although some girls do like things considered 'boy stuff', so don't just assume a girl isn't interested. There's no harm in asking if she likes something. In the same way, there are some things that are put in the girl basket that you might like to talk about, such as family or books. You might find

## COMMON INTERESTS

» favourite sport and sporting teams
» latest TV shows
» what's happening at school
» computer games and the latest techno stuff
» music you're listening to
» what your family is up to
» friends you have in common and new ones
» girls you think are hot
» boys she thinks are hot
» books you've read
» your pets and what they did
» funny stuff you've heard
» MySpace, Facebook, Twitter, YouTube
» food you like and have eaten
» movies you've seen or want to see
» cars you want to buy when you earn the money

## SOME OF THE THINGS YOU MIGHT TALK ABOUT WITH BOYS

» girls you think are hot
» sport
» computer games/TV shows/movies
» jokes (clean/dirty)
» great food/parties
» MySpace/Facebook/Twitter
» cars you would love to drive/own

that there are things you like talking about but other boys are not so interested in, and girls might be great to chat with on that particular subject. Because you're not competing with girls, they can be less judgemental than other boys. It works both ways too. Some girls find that guys are just better to hang out with as some teenage girls can be nasty to each other.

Choose what you talk about wisely—it can be really embarrassing if you say the wrong thing to a girl! If you think before you speak, you'll save yourself a lot of trouble. If you're stuck for something to talk about with a girl, try to find something she's interested in. Find subjects that are common to both boys and girls—you know, the boy stuff and girl stuff. This means something that everyone has in common, like music or movies— everyone likes some type of music or has seen at least one movie! Ask a girl what her favourite band is, or what type of music or movies she likes, or the worst movie she's ever seen.

## Secret boys' business

Some boy talk is not for girls' ears. You might feel pretty strongly about what's boys' business, not girls' business. As Harry (15) summed it up, 'There's limits on what you're going to say.' Boys aren't angels (and neither are girls) and there are times when you'll sit around and make jokes about dicks and boobs. That's totally normal, but you have to be careful about who hears those conversations. Another Year 10 boy told me, 'We're talking to [girls], "Hi, how are you", but on the inside we just want to get straight into them. But we treat the girls with respect.' A girl might feel uncomfortable if she heard you talking about how you'd love to grab that chick's arse, so don't say that kind of thing around her.

Boys have a right to privacy, just like everyone else. But girls

BOY TALK

**39**

can be kind of nosy. If a girl likes you and thinks you like another girl, she may well ask you questions about how you feel about that other girl, trying to find out whether you do like her. Tread carefully. When a girl asks 'What do you think of that girl?' or even 'What do you think of me?' you don't need to describe in detail her amazing breasts and what you'd like to do with them. Being 100 per cent honest might be taken as offensive, overly sexual or too much information; you might be better to play it safe. Don't just make up an answer you think she'll like either, as you can get it really wrong. Try to use 'safe' comments until you know the girl, something like 'She's pretty cute' or 'Oh, she's okay'. These are nice ways of putting it without appearing to be interested in the other girl, and it won't send the one you're with running.

When you know something is secret boys' business and you don't want to tell a girl, you're allowed to tell her that you don't want to discuss it. If a girl wants to know what you and your mates were chatting about, but you know she'll go crazy if you actually tell her, just explain that you don't feel comfortable talking about it. She might get upset or think you're hiding things from her, but if she's smart she'll understand. Let's face it, girls don't necessarily want boys to know everything they talk about to each other either.

All boys know that there are just certain things you can say in front of your mates that are not cool to say in front of girls. 'Sometimes we play a questionnaire: "What girl would you fuck in our year?" and sometimes my friend and I think, "Don't you wish all the girls in our year were sluts?",' Oliver (15) said. You probably already know that this is not the right thing to talk about in front of girls, but it can be easy to forget who you're talking to sometimes.

## ALL BOYS KNOW THAT THERE ARE JUST CERTAIN THINGS YOU CAN SAY IN FRONT OF YOUR MATES THAT ARE NOT COOL TO SAY IN FRONT OF GIRLS.

## THINGS GIRLS PROBABLY DON'T WANT TO HEAR

» if a girl is hot or not
» your ex, and how she compares with other girls
» boring details they're not interested in
» gross or offensive jokes
» stupid things you and your
mates did on the weekend
(unless it's a great story!)

GIRLS ARE
USUALLY PRETTY
INTERESTED TO
HEAR WHAT IT'S
LIKE LIVING IN THE
HEAD OF A BOY.

Remember, it's great to have female friends but be careful about considering her as your mate, just like any of your male friends. She is a girl and there are small differences between boys and girls. James (13) said, 'We've all got girls that are friends. They make us laugh sometimes, but we know they're just friends.' The difference between male friends, female friends and girlfriends may seem pretty obvious to you, but how different is the stuff you talk about, and the way you talk about it? It's important to remember who you're talking to, as even some male friends might find certain topics out of bounds. For instance, if someone is quite religious they may find talk about sex before marriage offensive. But with some girls you can say whatever you are thinking.

There's no strict rule when thinking about what topics are boy talk for boys' ears only. Girls are usually pretty interested to hear what it's like living in the head of a boy. Some girls even like toilet humour. 'It depends if the girl is like a boy's girl,' Dillon (15) explained to me. With other girls you might find you have to be careful about what you talk about and how you say things. If you really like a girl but you have to be a totally different person when you talk to her, you might want to reconsider if she's the right girl for you. Most guys find that their best female friends and their best girlfriends are people who let them be themselves. It's good to learn a bit of self-control around girls, but if you feel like she has gagged you, she might not be worth your time.

## Mates' ways

How you talk with your mates is just as important as what you talk about. Here are just a few of the ways that guys talk to each other.

*When to make a joke of it?* Talking between boys can seem more like a game of footy than a conversation. When you've got the ball, the attention is on you and you need to make a good pass or run with it. In groups of boys, you're either making a joke or setting someone else up to make a joke. 'We make each other laugh,' is how Connor (16) put it. Serious conversation is reserved for smaller groups or when it's just you and your best mate. Liam (17) told me, 'With my best friend I talk seriously about how I feel. One-on-one with many of my close friends I will talk seriously sometimes. In large groups it's all jokes, but through jokes we can still understand what each other's thoughts and feelings are.'

## THE WAY GUYS SAY THINGS TO EACH OTHER IS THROUGH JOKES TO HIDE HOW THEY'RE FEELING.

Even in large groups, many girls feel comfortable enough to discuss emotional or personal things. Boys are usually afraid that someone will rip them off if they bring up a serious topic while with their group of friends. Talking about a girl you like can be tough sometimes around a lot of mates because you're worried about what the other guys will think of you liking that girl. So a lot of the time the way guys say things to each other is through jokes to hide how they're feeling.

Girls love a joke but often there's a bit more honesty in how they talk. If girls want to talk about something serious they cut straight to it. This might be a bit surprising for a guy and may even throw you when a girl comes straight out and asks you what you think or how you feel about something. At the same time, girls might be a bit confused if you joke all the time and never say anything seriously. Rhys (13) said, 'You gotta be serious because they've got a short fuse sometimes. Not every girl. Some girls take it.'

***Who's top gun?*** 'Guys act differently around their mates. They try to be better than each other,' is how Jake (16) explained to me the competitive nature of males. A lot of the time the way

GUYS ACT DIFFERENTLY AROUND THEIR MATES.

they relate involves trying to outdo one each other, whether it's making the funniest joke, telling the weirdest story, making the most TV show references, doing voices, or just saying stuff that makes them look good. Guys challenge each other while they're talking.

Some guys are more competitive than others by nature, and not all guys like this way of communicating. If someone is going really overboard they could be accused of bragging. Or, if the guy is really trying to outdo his mates, he might put other people down, thinking it makes him look better next to them. Bear in mind, though, most girls don't like guys who show off heaps. Mitchell (15) told me it's not cool to be competitive in front of girls: 'You shouldn't bag each other out or put each other on

show.' It's fair enough to want to compete—that's part of how you get better at whatever you do, and also how you realise your strengths and weaknesses—but it's good to be able to chill out sometimes. To impress girls you need to be able to show them that there's more to you than just wanting to be the best all the time.

***There's grunting and then there's . . .*** When you next talk to your friends, take a note of the different ways they use words or sentences. When chatting to mates you may find yourself saying clipped and straight-to-the-point phrases rather than whole sentences, and they may not be very long conversations. Some people call this 'grunting', and teenage boys are famous for it. A phone call between you and friend might go something like this:

## 'YOU WOULDN'T PICK YOUR NOSE IN FRONT OF A GIRL . . .'

Mate: 'Wanna come to the park?'
You: 'Yep. When?'
Mate: 'Six.
You: 'Okay. See ya.'

This might work well between you and your male friends, but other people will want you to give more detail. When your mum asks how school was, she wants you to tell her more than 'Good', 'Bad', or 'Okay'. When your teacher asks you to do a speech on a book you read, you have to give it in longer sentences. If you want to attract a girl's interest, be prepared for her wanting to know more about you. It's hard to get to know someone if they only speak in one-syllable words and two-word sentences. So think about how you use language when you're talking to a girl and loosen up and be more expressive.

## IT CAN BE GREAT FUN TO OUT GROSS YOUR MATES.

## IT'S HARD TO GET TO KNOW SOMEONE IF THEY ONLY SPEAK IN ONE-SYLLABLE WORDS AND TWO-WORD SENTENCES.

*Ah, gross!* Boys are made of slugs and snails and puppy dog tails. They love being gross. It can be great fun to out gross your mates—there's that competitive nature again. But can you behave like this in front of everyone you know? As Mason (16) put it, 'You wouldn't pick your nose if front of a girl and eat it.' You might not do this in front of your mates either, but there are probably some gross things boys get up to that they wouldn't want girls to see. Some guys don't care as another Year 10 told me, 'We've got one mate who'll say anything. "Aw, I gotta crack a fart." And he'll pull his pants down and show his arse. In front of girls! If you don't like it then stuff you. He's being himself. He wants to make people laugh.' If you want to be yourself, uncensored and uncut, in front of anyone, that's your choice. All girls fart too, that's a fact, and some girls love being gross. But you need to be flexible, depending on the company you keep. It's not a good look for all, and it could put you in a bad light if the girl you want to talk to finds it off-putting.

# 3 STRANGE CREATURES CALLED GIRLS

Perhaps you've read about them, or spotted them moving in packs through the schoolyard. Girls! They seem like strange, exotic animals and you really don't understand them, or so you think. Nobody ever really tells you what girls are like, or what they're into. You pick up clues from TV shows, but those aren't real girls, just characters. Boys with teenage sisters may be wiser, but then again, they only see the side of her that hogs the bathroom for hours and talks on the phone all night. Your friends can be good for information, but you might just all be in the same position: you don't really understand them, and don't even know where to begin!

## The gift of the gab

Talking to girls is a little bit different than talking to your mates. One of the main differences is communication styles. For instance, girls are likely to talk a lot more than boys. Sometimes it seems like they can go on for hours. Boys often say only what is required. They don't talk for fun like girls do. If you're in a conversation with a girl, it may seem like she's running the show. Suddenly you've turned into a giant pair of ears to listen to all her problems. This

## TALKING TO GIRLS IS A LITTLE BIT DIFFERENT THAN TALKING TO YOUR MATES. FOR INSTANCE . . . GIRLS ARE LIKELY TO TALK A LOT MORE THAN BOYS.

can get kind of boring, especially if you're used to joking around when you talk.

Boy conversations tend to be like a tennis match: one boy hits the ball, the other boy hits back. Sometimes you gain points for good jokes. Sometimes you miss the ball. Girl conversations are kind of like gymnastics: the girl does a series of complicated tricks and then sits down and waits for the next girl to perform. Girls enjoy talking for long periods of time. But when they're talking to other girls, they know when to pause and let the other girl tell their own story or give their own opinion. But when boys and girls start talking to each other, things get a bit weird: the rules of two different games are being played at the same time.

If the girl dominates the conversation, she might talk for a while, then pause and wait for your input, but if you give your usual short and to-the-point answer, she's going to feel pretty confused. Same goes if the boy dominates the conversation— he might say something, wait for a response from the girl, and then cut her off because he doesn't know how to deal with a long answer. But how do you win the game when the rules aren't clear?

The secret is compromise: a whole new game must be created so that boys and girls can communicate. This doesn't mean that we should all be timing our conversations and programming talking time. We'll leave that sort of thing to talk-show TV. What it means is trying to understand how girls play the talking game, and trying to learn their rules as well as teaching them your own. Sometimes you'll play by their rules—being a good listener never hurt anyone. But sitting around talking about yourself for hours can be pretty boring. That's where you need to step in and show her how boys talk—have a bit of verbal fun. Pick up the pace of the game and play something new. Girls like having fun conversations too!

Girls and boys have a lot in common—we're all human beings, not aliens. Learning girl talk really isn't that difficult. It just takes a little patience and understanding. As Scotty (12) summed it up, 'You gotta talk to girls and see what they're like.' Be a good listener and a good team player. But don't be shy about teaching a girl how to talk boy talk.

STRANGE CREATURES CALLED GIRLS

GIRLS YOUR OWN AGE ARE EXPERIENCING
THAT CRAZY THING CALLED PUBERTY.

# THE BEST WAY TO BE UNDERSTANDING OF GIRLS' CHANGES IS TO KNOW YOUR FACTS.

## It's a body thing

Another thing to remember is that, like you, girls your own age are experiencing that crazy thing called puberty. They are starting to look different—some of them might already look more like women than children. Puberty means change: for your body, your brain, and also for your rights and responsibilities. Boys and girls both experience these changes in their own time. Think about how you are changing and what you are feeling. One good way to work this out is to ask yourself, 'Am I more interested in hanging out with my mates or dating girls?'

The best way to be understanding of girls' changes is to know your facts. Girls are usually a little ahead of us guys in the puberty stakes. Most girls start to go through puberty between eight and 13 years of age. Their breasts start off as little buds underneath their nipples—at this stage, a lot of girls start wearing 'training bras', which is like the more developed bra's little sister. Girls also get pubic hair, like guys do, and for them those potentially embarrassing short, dark and curlies will eventually cover the outer labia (folds of skin around the vagina).

One of the biggest deals for girls is menstruation, aka periods.

# 'ONCE I WAS TALKING TO A GIRL AND SHE SAID, "SORRY I WAS BEING A BITCH LAST WEEK".'

It may come as a surprise, but girls and women have monthly cycles that prepare them for having babies. An egg, or ova, is released, then the womb lining builds up to make it all soft and cushy for the baby. But when the egg isn't fertilised, women's bodies know they don't need that extra padding in the womb, and the womb lining and egg are slowly expelled from the body through the vagina over several days. Sounds gross but, like wet dreams, it's natural, right?

## ONE OF THE BIGGEST DEALS FOR GIRLS IS MENSTRUATION, AKA PERIODS.

As you can imagine, all these changes can make a girl feel emotional, so don't get annoyed when girls are bitchy or rude sometimes! There's a thing called premenstrual tension (PMT)— it's also called premenstrual syndrome or stress (PMS) —and it's often part of menstruation. Laura (14) explained PMS as 'When you get heaps annoyed when you have your periods.' Zac (16) told me, 'Once I was talking to a girl and she said, "Sorry I was being a bitch last week." I said why, and she said, "I had PMS." It explains

## ALL THESE CHANGES CAN MAKE A GIRL FEEL EMOTIONAL, SO DON'T GET ANNOYED WHEN GIRLS ARE BITCHY OR RUDE SOMETIMES!

a little.' Basically, the levels of hormones in a girl's body change during her cycle and this can mean that sometimes girls feel more sensitive then than at other times. Some girls experience this a lot, some not so much. So as you can see, there are plenty of things to learn about how women's bodies work—I suggest you pay attention in health class and biology, or do a bit of reading in the library. The more you know the more you can understand what they are going through.

## That touchy-feely thing

Girls also hug and kiss each other . . . a lot. It seems at almost any opportunity they'll throw their arms around each other for a nice big bear hug. But why do they hug like they're never going to see each other again? Girls tend to be more physically close to their friends than boys are to their friends. When girls are best friends, they often like to hug, play with each other's hair, do each other's makeup and stuff like that. When girls trust each other, they like to show their affection in a physical way. Boys hug too, sometimes, but only if they feel very comfortable.

Sometimes girls want to hug boys who are their friends, not

BOYS GET INTO FISTFIGHTS,
BUT GIRLS NORMALLY FIGHT
WITH WORDS INSTEAD—
A GOOD OLD CAT FIGHT.

boyfriends. This might feel a bit weird if you're only used to getting hugs off your mum. But just relax—a hug is a nice way of showing that two people are friends and they feel close to each other. If you feel awkward about body contact, just remember that someone who's your friend, and willing to hug you, is also not going to judge you.

On the other side of the coin, girls bitch about their friends and end up fighting with them. Why, when it seems perfectly obvious they are good friends? Well, we all have a certain amount of built-up energy that we need to get out of our system and this can come out as aggression. Most adults have learnt to control these emotions, blowing them off in healthy ways, like going to the gym or a long run. But when you're young, it's hard to know what to do with pent-up energy. Because boys are encouraged to be sporty and physically active, a lot of boys let off steam by playing sport, which is a great way to deal with it. A lot of girls play sport too, but some girls don't. When boys and girls don't have healthy ways of venting their aggression, they can turn it on the people around them. Boys get into fistfights, but girls normally fight with words instead—a good old cat fight.

Perhaps one of the reasons girls fight with their friends is because they know that most of the time they can and will make up afterwards. The emotional rollercoaster of fighting, hating each other for a while and then making up releases a lot of energy. If you fought with someone you didn't like, there wouldn't be an emotional resolution at the end—just more fighting! It may seem strange, but it's one of those things that girls do when they're younger, but hopefully grow out of as they get older and know how to handle their emotions better. The best thing to do is stay out of the way. Try not to get between two girls having a verbal stoush because you don't need to engage in anyone else's fight. Sometimes that's easier said than done and, if you do end up being part of it, bear in mind it will pass. Female besties do have a habit of making up.

## Shop-a-holics

I know what you're thinking: hours of going in and out of shops, trying on piles of clothes and looking at yourself in the mirror—it's a day in hell. Most boys probably still get their mums to buy their clothes! But for girls, going out with friends to try on clothes and makeup is a fun social outing, and it can also give them a confidence boost to have their best buds around to tell them what looks great on them. It is a bit of a generalisation as not all girls like shopping, but many do! A lot of teenage girls are into shopping and having sleepovers and talking constantly with their girl friends—girls are natural communicators.

Don't be put off by how girls travel in packs, yakking away. All they're doing is building communication skills that will help them later in life. You can even benefit from trying to keep up in a conversation with girls—we all live in a world where communication technology rules.

If you're still thinking that girls are more like aliens than human beings and that they come from a different planet—men are from Mars, women are from Venus type of thing—you might want to ask yourself, 'Do I understand girls?' Maybe you tried to chat up a girl and were rejected almost straightaway. What is with that? The truth is that girls and boys aren't really that different, but there are a few little differences that count in a big way.

A LOT OF TEENAGE GIRLS ARE INTO SHOPPING AND HAVING SLEEPOVERS AND TALKING CONSTANTLY WITH THEIR GIRL FRIENDS—GIRLS ARE NATURAL COMMUNICATORS.

# 4 GETTING TO KNOW HER

You probably feel it's safer to stay clear of girls if you think they are strange animals. But once your hormones kick in, you'll notice girls even more. Even if you don't want to start going out with girls right now, it's good to try and understand them. You need to, really, because boys and girls share a lot of the same habitat. Guys who have friends that are girls know that girl friends are different to guy friends. It's a whole other kind of relationship from the one you have with your male mates. You tend to do different things together and talk about other stuff. There are girls who like doing the same things guys do, like computer games or surfing, and that's cool as it takes the pressure off you needing to learn how to do girl stuff. And there are also lots of things out there that you can do that aren't actually guy or girl specific, like going to the movies. So not having anything in common is no excuse not to think about girls as friends.

## You go girl friend

Girls and guys can be great friends, even if they don't want to 'go out' or kiss or whatever. You'll find that being friends with a girl helps you understand girls better—there's nothing like firsthand evidence. Maybe a girl friend will even help you get a girlfriend (and do note the difference in the spelling here, as they are not the same). You'll just need to make sure your girl friend doesn't have feelings for you as you could hurt her if you go out with another girl if she does. You need to make sure that both of you are 'just friends'.

## GIRLS AND GUYS CAN BE GREAT FRIENDS, EVEN IF THEY DON'T WANT TO 'GO OUT' OR KISS OR WHATEVER.

This can be tough because a lot of the time teenagers hide their feelings from each other. She may even lie when she says she doesn't like you 'that way', so you need to be clear on the rules, even if you have to say, 'We're just friends.' Your relationship might become something more later on or you just stay good mates together; either way, you need to find out where both of you stand, right from the start.

Girls who are friends with guys like to feel they belong with you and with your mates, but they don't necessarily want to become

## 'IF SHE COMES TO YOU WHEN YOU'RE WITH YOUR FRIENDS, SHE'LL GET TEASED.'

just one of the guys. This part's tricky: you need to make sure she feels comfortable in your group, but also give her respect as a girl. Sarah (17) commented, 'Most girls don't like to be one of the boys and just want to be treated as a female. Like, they don't want to rough house around or talk about boy things. They want to be girly.' Most often you'll find it's as Cameron (13) says, 'If she comes to you when you're with your friends, she'll get teased. She comes to you when you're alone.' When you're hanging out with a girl, don't let your mates harass her. If you're introducing a female friend to your mates, it's your job to protect her. She might feel vulnerable, especially if she's the only girl there. Don't let your friends make jokes about her or say sexist things about women. At the same time, don't ignore her. Try to find something that she and your mates have in common. If it doesn't work out, you might want to try hanging out alone with her. Some of your mates just may not be ready to be friends with girls.

Once you make friends with a girl, you might be worried about where to go and what to do. You don't want it to be a date if you're just friends. A good place to start is at your place or hers. Watch a movie with her family, or play music you both like. You probably have something in common, or you wouldn't be friends, so try to focus on that if you're stuck for ideas. Maybe she likes the same bands as you, so listening to music together or seeing the band play live or going shopping together for band merchandise are all good ideas. Do the same kind of things with her that you'd do with a mate, but keep in mind that she's a girl. Maybe she might like to go for a bike ride with you, but don't expect her to want to do extreme mountain-bike riding if you and your guy mates do that. Respect what she wants, and you will get on pretty well.

## Talking nicely

Isaac (15) summed up the difference between the way guys talk to each other and how they talk to girls: 'If it was him and a chick, he'd talk differently and say things that he doesn't tell his boys.' When I asked a group of Year 8 boys whether it was different talking to girls they said: 'A lot different. You're shy. You're speechless. You say one word, then a few seconds later you think of something. You plan your words. When you're talking to your mates you slur a little bit but when you talk to a girl you have to talk nicely.'

# HOW CAN YOU TELL IF A GIRL LIKES YOU AS MORE THAN A FRIEND?

Talking nicely is something that girls like and there are a number of ways you can do that when you want to chat to a girl you really like. Yes, it is different, but if you want to talk to girls you need to put away those boy ways and interact so that she becomes interested in you.

## Reading the signals

How can you tell if a girl likes you as more than a friend? Communication isn't just about words—body language and tone of voice are a huge part of it. It's easy to get really confused if you don't read the signals right. 'Sometimes they pass notes to you,' is how Nathan (12) told me he knew when they liked him. But if you're not getting a clear message through what she does, you might need to look at what she says and how she says it.

Sometimes a girl says something, but really she means something else. Trying to find out if a girl likes you can be like trying to solve a cryptic crossword. You've got all the hints, but they don't make sense, and can even make you more confused than before! Being in tune with a girl's signals is tricky, but you need to give it a shot. At least if you make an attempt to understand

## TIPS FOR TALKING WITH GIRLS

» Use a friendly tone of voice.

» Don't swear.

» Don't slur your words.

» Use a soft tone of voice.

» Pause when you talk to give her room to say things.

» Look her in the eyes while you talk.

» Don't yell at her across the room.

» Smile while you talk.

» Let her speak first.

## BODY LANGUAGE

» mannerisms
» postures
» facial expressions
» tone of voice

her, she might be more willing to lend you a hand. Body language is about how mannerisms, postures and facial expressions show what someone's really thinking. Picking up on negative or positive vibes has a lot to do with reading body language.

*Mannerisms:* Everyone has quirky things that we do, almost without noticing. Things like biting your fingernails, sniffing, pushing your hair behind your ears or looking at your watch. A lot of the time, people do these things when they're nervous. If a girl does a particular thing while she's talking to you, she might be feeling a bit uncomfortable. So be sensitive to her feelings if you want to get to know her more.

SOMETIMES A GIRL SAYS SOMETHING, BUT REALLY SHE MEANS SOMETHING ELSE.

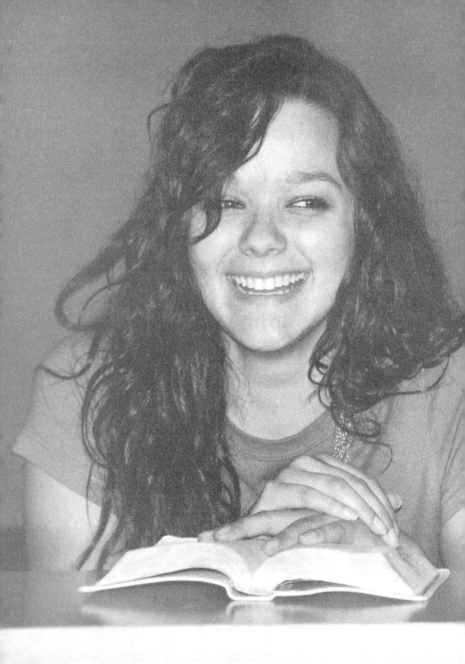

# BODY LANGUAGE IS ABOUT HOW MANNERISMS, POSTURES AND FACIAL EXPRESSIONS SHOW WHAT SOMEONE'S REALLY THINKING.

*Postures:* If she folds her arms, hunches over or turns away from you when you try and talk to her then she's probably not interested. If she doesn't look you in the eye, talks quietly or looks into the distance a lot, but smiles sometimes, then she might just be a bit shy. If she sits facing towards you, looks you in the eye, and sneaks a peek at you when you're looking the other way, then she probably likes you!

*Facial expressions:* Obviously, the big one to look out for is smiling—if she smiles and laughs a lot, then you're doing well! But more subtle expressions like looking puzzled, questioning or critical can be a bit hard to read. Look at what her eyes are doing: if they're bright and focused, she's interested. If they seem a bit dull, or narrow from time to time, she might be bored. If she doesn't look interested but she hasn't walked away yet, you should ask her how she's feeling—she'll be impressed that you picked up on her not feeling 100 per cent.

*Tone of voice:* Your mum or dad has probably said this to you before: It's not what you say, it's how you say it. If a girl says things in a sarcastic or bored tone of voice, you're probably not doing it for her. But a lot of people think it's cool to always sound sarcastic, even if you mean something, so don't take it too personally. If she's being really sarcastic, she's probably teasing you. Look for tone of voice when she's upset: sometimes girls will try to avoid conflict by telling you that everything's okay. But if she doesn't sound entirely convinced by what she's saying, you might want to ask her what she really feels.

Sometimes girls get pretty nervous talking to guys. It's a good idea to be aware of the signals you are sending to her. Try to reassure her with positive body language: sit or stand in an open and relaxed way. Don't cross your arms or legs because it's sending the message that you don't want to interact. Try not to eyeball her, but make sure you look at her from time to time. If you feel weird about looking her in the eye, just look at her ear or just past her head, and it will have the same effect as eye contact (unless you're right in front of her face, in which case there's really nothing else to do but have some long, meaningful eye contact). Don't sit too close, unless she seems really keen. The easiest way to turn a girl off is to get in her personal space when she doesn't want it. And just try to feed off her vibes: if she's relaxed, interested and giving you plenty of attention, then you're further than you think in talking terms.

## Getting to know her

How do you get to know a girl, let alone make friends with her when she always seems to travel in female packs, even to the toilets? They talk about girl stuff and act like they wouldn't touch you with a ten-metre stick. Plus, if girls want to be friends with guys, it's never you, right? They only want to talk to the cool guy, but he's not giving away any of his girl secrets to other guys, so what can you do? It's simple really. Make sure you understand why girls want to be with boys, and think about your way of communicating. Sometimes it seems like boys and girls talk totally different languages. When you try to speak her language, she just laughs at your bad accent. So how do you become fluent in girl talk?

*What does she like doing?:* This may seem obvious, but

## SOMETIMES GIRLS GET PRETTY NERVOUS TALKING TO GUYS.

finding out more about her can help with making conversation, as getting to know her better is the whole point, right? You can begin by asking around but, whatever you do, don't stalk her! Just try to get the answers to a few questions: Does she love English or hate it? Does she go in races at swimming carnivals? Does she catch the bus or train after school? If she doesn't go to your school, see what you can find out about the school. Do you know anyone who goes there? This info can be used as conversation starters when you get talking to her. That way, when you have the guts to go up and say 'Hi', you'll be a little better prepared. The last thing you want is to get stuck and have to talk about the weather.

*Don't ask 'yes' or 'no' questions.* Lots of girls love to talk, but you still need to ask the right questions. Asking something that has a 'yes' or 'no' answer is guaranteed to sink the boat and leave you stranded. Asking general questions like 'What did you do on the weekend?' will give her the chance to tell you a few things about herself and what she likes to do. If you ask, 'Was your weekend good?' you'll probably get a simple 'yes' or 'no' and then you'll have to think of another question. Don't make things so hard for yourself, instead ask her, 'What did you do on

# SOMETIMES IT SEEMS LIKE BOYS AND GIRLS TALK TOTALLY DIFFERENT LANGUAGES.

the weekend?' This opens up the conversation and means you won't have to throw too many questions at her in a short space of time.

*Tell her something about yourself.* She's probably just as interested in finding out about you as you are about her. Maybe you think that your weekend was pretty boring, but if she's just told you about her weekend, then she'll want to hear some news from you. Girls trade stories—when one girl says something about herself, another girl will talk about something similar that she experienced. It's called relating, and it's something that boys need to learn if they want to speak girl talk. Think of it like tennis: one person serves, the other hits back, like a question and an answer. But you have to remember to keep hitting back, or the game will be over. Even if your weekend was boring, don't just say 'It was boring'—that's really boring! Give her some details, explain why it was boring, and then tell her what the best weekend ever would be like. Maybe it would be doing something with her!

*Find out what she likes.* Having something in common with a girl is great—that way you have more to talk about and less awkward silences. But you probably think that most girls don't

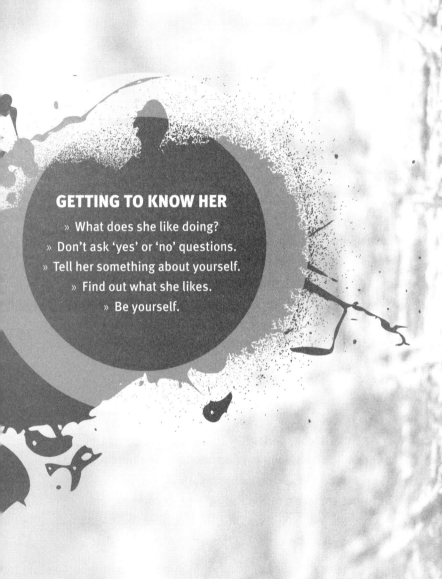

## GETTING TO KNOW HER

» What does she like doing?
» Don't ask 'yes' or 'no' questions.
» Tell her something about yourself.
» Find out what she likes.
» Be yourself.

like cars, surfing, extreme sport and video games. Well, you'd be surprised. Make sure you find out what she likes. Perhaps you like surfing but she likes walking on the beach—they're different things, but you can still find a common interest: the beach. Ask her what she likes about the beach, which beaches are her favourite, and whether she's ever tried surfing. If you guys have absolutely nothing in common, don't freak out. It doesn't mean you won't get on very well. All you have to do is show an interest in what she likes. Maybe she likes shopping, makeup and clothes (like most girls, right?) but there is usually something unique about girls that they don't always advertise. You never know, she could introduce you to something you never thought you'd like.

*Be yourself.* Most guys want to impress girls. They might act tough or cool, brag about stuff they did or didn't do, or do dangerous things to show how brave they are. Think about it. If your best mate was showing off, exaggerating or behaving like an idiot, would you think he was cool? Probably not. It's easy for you to tell when your mates are behaving differently. But it's just as easy for girls to see when a guy is not being himself, especially in conversation. Remember to be yourself and that will win you friends, both guys and girls. It takes a lot of effort to try and be someone you're not, so give yourself a break. Don't try too hard and girls will respect you for being genuine. Plus, you're more likely to meet girls that you click with if you are not trying to be someone else.

# What not to do

Girls can be confusing. One minute they're laughing at your jokes and the next they seem to be going psycho at you for no reason! You might want to blame it on PMS but the truth is girls can be sensitive about what boys say to them or do around them simply because they like the guy and don't want to be made fun of in front of him. They're human too, and feel just as insecure as you do. If you want to have girls as friends, you need to be considerate of their feelings, just as you would a guy.

Joking around is a good way to get talking to girls—boys and girls appreciate a sense of humour—and it can be a great way to break the ice if you're nervous about talking to a girl. But inappropriate or rude jokes, or jokes made at the expense of others are just not on. When you're hanging out with your mates, they probably find it funny when you make jokes about girls. After all, girls' bodies are changing and it may seem like an easy target to joke about breast changes, periods or body hair. But although they look like they're 100 per cent in control, girls are just as freaked out about their bodies developing as boys are about wet dreams and body odour.

## ONE MINUTE THEY'RE LAUGHING AT YOUR JOKES AND THE NEXT THEY SEEM TO BE GOING PSYCHO AT YOU FOR NO REASON!

It can sometimes be a fine line you have to walk, but it's important to be aware of the kind of things that girls just won't stand for. Here's what you should not do when talking to a girl.

***Don't make jokes about the way she looks.*** Most girls are super aware of how they look. The last thing they need is some boy pointing out their pimples, leg hair, developing breasts or how they keep sneaking off to the bathroom every hour. It's hard enough going through puberty without someone laughing about what we can't control. Just remember, the next time you make a joke about someone's pimples, it might come around to bite you because at some point you will get your own dose of face craters.

***Don't make rude, sexist or inappropriate jokes or comments.*** Your mates might think that blonde jokes or 'your momma' jokes are great, but girls probably think otherwise. Sexist jokes or comments are when you say something about a woman that makes fun of her sex, body or her sexuality. Making sexist jokes about other girls or women when you're talking to a girl is not cool—even if it's not about her, the girl you're talking to may feel upset or offended. Jayden (13) said, 'Some boys don't know what girls want. You have to give

## WHAT NOT TO DO

» Make jokes about the way she looks.
» Make rude, sexist or inappropriate
jokes or comments.
» Use sexist words or phrases.
» Be her friend when you're alone
together, then tease her when
you're with your mates.
» Do gross things.
» Be a bully.

## GIRLS ARE JUST AS FREAKED OUT ABOUT THEIR BODIES DEVELOPING AS BOYS ARE ABOUT WET DREAMS AND BODY ODOUR.

respect to get respect. It means don't be rude, if you're getting respect from someone then you know they're treating you well, and you should treat them the same.' Sexist jokes show that you don't respect women, and you know what girls want: R-E-S-P-E-C-T!

*Don't use sexist words or phrases.* It's a fact that boys and girls both swear but there are some words that are not okay to use. Words like slut, whore, ho, tits and pussy can all be seen as sexist. When you use these words, even if you're not being serious, you can still hurt a girl's feelings. Rappers talk about booty but that doesn't mean you can too. If you use sexist words when you're talking to a girl, you might make her feel uncomfortable, or make her think that you're a sicko.

*Don't be her friend when you're alone together, then tease her when you're with your mates.* It's hard to juggle being friends with guys and being friends with girls, especially if there are no girls in your group. But acting two different ways can make girls really mad. Teasing a girl may win points with your male friends, but it's just going to be confusing for your female friends. If being cool for your mates is more important than being friends with girls, then don't lead a girl on by acting two different ways. Decide what you

JOKING AROUND IS A GOOD WAY
TO GET TALKING TO GIRLS.

want—if it's friendship with girls then don't worry about what your mates think. They're probably just jealous that you have the guts to talk to girls anyway.

*Don't do gross things.* There are plenty of girls who enjoy burping competitions and plenty of guys who don't like swearing and always wash their hands before dinner. Good manners are important skills to learn and it's not like you have to be a well-behaved mumma's boy around girls. Some girls wouldn't even be into guys like that. But it's good to know when it's appropriate to have good manners and when you can kick back and forget about that stuff. Sam (13) told me that gross behaviours shouldn't be displayed in front of girls: 'Don't smoke, burp, fart, anything rude, anything dumb, don't be a fool, don't be dirty, don't eat, don't chew with your mouth open, don't do drugs, don't act like a nerd.' If you want a girl to like you it's probably a good idea to avoid being repulsive. That kind of stuff might impress your mates, but it probably won't impress girls. As Jarrod (12) said, 'Our heads have got girls in there now, we have to improve our behaviour.' He's got the right idea.

*Don't be a bully.* When teasing becomes a regular thing, it's called bullying. This is really, really not on. You might think that you were just mucking around, but when teasing develops into bullying, it's serious stuff. Bullying can cause girls (and guys) to become depressed, to self-harm, and to change schools to escape the fire. Think about what you're going to say before you say it—would you like it if someone called your mum a slut, or teased your sister about her hairy armpits, or made rude jokes about your female cousins? Probably not. Words are powerful things, especially for girls, and you may be surprised to find out just how much your words can hurt. As Connor (13) said, 'If you see a girl crying, you give her a hug, comfort her, show that you have a feeling.' If you try to impress your mates by bullying girls, they will probably have a hissy fit or freeze you out. When girls get upset it's usually for a reason. Think about what you might have said to make her angry, and remember to not say or do it again.

## Are you sending the right message?

Guys and girls have a lot more ways to communicate now than people did in the past. Technology like SMS, emailing and instant messaging just didn't exist when your parents were your age.

## GUYS AND GIRLS HAVE A LOT MORE WAYS TO COMMUNICATE NOW THAN PEOPLE DID IN THE PAST.

New technology can make communicating really easy and fun, especially if you're a bit shy. You should, Matt (12) says, 'Call her or email, but mostly girls give you their emails. Lots of times you can say things in emails you wouldn't say face to face.' But there can be hassles with technology, as one boy pointed out, 'MSN. That's how fights start sometimes.' Technology can provide you with opportunities you wouldn't have in everyday life: 'It's a good way to communicate on MSN. If you call them, their parents ask who's calling. They ask too many questions.' But it shouldn't replace face-to-face talking—it's pretty important to be able to communicate without technology. Because the technology is fairly new, people are still trying to work out the 'do's' and 'dont's' of it. Like communicating face-to-face, there are certain things that will be personal preferences. Everyone has a different idea about what they like or don't like. But if you really have no clue what to say and what not to say when using communication technology, the following tips should help:

IT'S PRETTY IMPORTANT TO
BE ABLE TO COMMUNICATE
WITHOUT TECHNOLOGY.

# Emails

DO:

- be friendly, open and honest
- tell them things about yourself, what you've been up to, etc.
- use words you would normally use
- ask questions
- answer questions she asked in a previous email
- tell jokes or funny stories
- keep them at a medium length—three sentences is too little, three pages is way too much, but three paragraphs is about the right amount
- check your email about once a week, or more often
- answer emails in around two to six days.

DON'T:

- type in capitals ALL THE TIME
- include too much nerdy stuff—geekspeak is not for everyone
- answer her long email in three words or dot points—she might feel like you don't care enough to write a decent length email in reply
- leave her email sitting in your inbox unanswered for weeks
- harass her if she hasn't replied as soon as you'd like her to.

# SMS or text messaging

DO:

- use it to get in contact with her or see how she's going
- use it to flirt—tell her you're thinking about her
- text how you would talk, not what's considered cool
- use words you feel comfortable with—if you don't want to call her 'babe' you don't have to
- reply to her message the same day you get it, or the day after
- send an email instead if what you want to say is longer, or call if you need her input straightaway.

DON'T:

- send her messages at all hours of the day or night
- use it to keep track of where she is 24/7—she has a right to her own business
- send anything you'd be embarrassed about if someone read it—people can lose their phones or have them stolen, or even taken away by a teacher
- send messages that are so long they take two or three different messages to send
- spend heaps of money on phone credit—sometimes there are things that can wait until you see each other in person, which is free (if you live close or go to the same school)
- make the mistake of sending a text message to the person that the text message was about—take your time when sending a message and make sure you send it to the right person!
- break up via text messaging—it's really not a good idea.

# MSN and instant messaging

DO:

- arrange to meet her online, or ask what time she's normally online
- chat how you would normally chat face-to-face
- keep conversations short—30 minutes is a good amount of time before things start to get boring
- share links to funny or interesting things you've found online
- use emoticons to express yourself
- make jokes
- ask questions.

DON'T:

- spend hours waiting around for her to come online
- send her heaps of messages if her status is Away or Busy—if she wants to talk she'll let you know
- talk about other people in a bad way—you never know who could be reading, and MSN history can be saved
- have multiple windows open and be talking about her with someone else at the same time—it's easy to get your windows mixed up and send the wrong message to her
- communicate all your emotions via emoticons—sometimes it's better to just tell her how you feel in words
- talk about heavy issues—MSN fights are very quick to start because people feel less confronted when the actual person is not in front of them; and MSN fights can be just as damaging as face-to-face fights, perhaps even more so because your words can be saved and read again later!

## MySpace and Facebook

DO:

- add her as a friend and check out her profile and pictures
- comment on any pictures you like
- write on her wall if you have something to say
- send her free gifts or use applications (on Facebook) like Hatching Eggs to send her something cute
- invite her to events via the site
- send an email through the site if you have something longer or more personal you want to discuss
- post any photos or videos of her—if she's camera-shy, ask her permission first.

DON'T:

- spend every waking minute checking your feed to see if she's done anything new
- use the website as an excuse for stalking her—most people will be turned off by that
- make a large number of comments or send a large number of gifts—she might feel crowded
- comment on every single photo—it's nice to have admirers, but save your comments for one or two photos you really like
- reply straightaway to her messages or comments—she might think you don't have anything else to do.

Above all, remember nice guys don't always finish last; in fact, being a nice guy might win you some new female friends.

## Healthy and unhealthy relationships

There is one thing a healthy relationship is based on, and that is RESPECT. You know that you are in a healthy relationship with someone because you feel good about yourself when you are around that person. Unhealthy relationships can make you feel sad, angry, scared or worried.

You should feel safe around the other person and feel that you can trust her with your secrets. In a healthy relationship, you like to spend time with the other person, instead of feeling like you're pressured into spending time with them. Unhealthy relationships do not include trust and respect, which are very important parts of a friendship, or dating relationship. No one deserves to be in an unhealthy relationship.

Relationships are about mutual respect. In any relationship you have the right to expect to share equally in decision making. If the other person always makes decisions about where you will go and who you will spend time with, then this could be an indicator of someone who likes to have power and control in a relationship.

Disagreements might still happen, but you learn to stay

## A HEALTHY RELATIONSHIP

» You have fun together.

» You both feel able to be yourself.

» You have a friendship, not just a physical relationship.

» You can have differing opinions and interests without being pressured to change your mind.

» You listen to each other.

» You both compromise, say sorry, and talk arguments out.

» You don't have to spend all your time together; you can spend time alone or with friends or family.

## EXAMPLES OF ABUSE

» *Emotional*—puts you down, calls
you names.
» *Physical*—hurts you or threatens
to hurt you.
» *Sexual*—touches you or forces or tricks you
to do sexual things that you don't want to do.
» *Financial*—controls your money and
how you spend it.
» *Social*—controls your contact
with friends or family.

calm and talk about how you feel. Talking calmly helps you to understand the real reason for not getting along, and it's much easier to figure out how to fix it.

When someone treats you badly, it can be very hurtful. A warning sign that your relationship may be abusive is when a person tries to control or hurt another person.

Relationships take time, energy, and care to make them healthy. The relationships that you make in your teen years will be a special part of your life and will teach you some of the most important lessons about who you are.

# 5 THE DATING GAME

Most of us learn about 'dating' from American movies and TV shows. Usually a boy asks a girl to go out to dinner and a movie, then takes her home and kisses her when on the front porch before she goes inside. But everything in Hollywood isn't exactly like real life. Sometimes a date can be more like a sitcom than a romance. If it's bad enough, it can even turn into a horror!

In Australia, we don't really date like Americans do—we usually only see one person at a time, rather than a few different people. So when someone says, 'Do you want to go out with me?', they often mean more than 'Do you want to share a pizza with me?' More likely what they're saying is, 'Do you want to be my boyfriend (or girlfriend)?' Of course this means a lot of people get together then break up, and when you're still a teenager, breaking up is not always a big deal. You might go out with a girl for two weeks and then break up. As you get a bit older, things might get a bit more long term—it might take at least two months or two years for that to happen.

## HOLLYWOOD ISN'T EXACTLY LIKE REAL LIFE.

## SOME GUYS ACTUALLY FIND MASTURBATING BEFORE A DATE HELPS CALM THEIR NERVES.

## Banish those annoying butterflies

The risk with going on a date, or starting to 'see' someone more often, is that it won't work out. If you really want to be with a girl more than once, and you're going on your first date, it can be pretty scary. A lot of people suffer from nerves before a big date. You don't want to be a bundle of nerves when you meet her so it's a good idea to do something to help you calm down beforehand:

* Do something physical—kick a soccer ball, go for a swim or lift weights.
* If you're not into sport, you can try slow breathing (not deep breathing, just slow!)—breathe in for three seconds, then out for three seconds. Slow breathing is a great way to help you calm down, and you can do it for ten minutes right before you meet her.
* You might also like to try meditating, or praying if you are religious, as this usually helps people to clear their minds and relax.

You might have heard jokes on TV about masturbating before a date, but some guys actually do this and find that it helps them calm their nerves!

## YOU'LL PROBABLY BE SCARED THAT YOU'LL SCREW IT UP SOMEHOW AND MAKE HER HATE YOU FOREVER.

Basically, do whatever makes you less anxious and don't forget she probably has butterflies too. This is one of the fun things about going on a date: being really excited about seeing each other. A little bit of nerves is good, but not so much that you're totally awkward around each other!

## First impressions last . . . or do they?

Lots of people say that first impressions count as they impact on the way someone thinks about you. This can be pretty daunting if you're on a first date with a girl you really like. You've plucked up the courage to ask her out (or maybe you're flattered because she asked you out) and you want to make a good impression. You have to look your best, say the right things, and take her to the right place. It's a lot to think about! And you'll probably be scared that you'll screw it up somehow and make her hate you forever.

Wait a moment. Think about someone you like—a friend, teacher, or distant relative—and ask yourself, did you love them as soon as you met them? A lot of people don't like each other when they first meet, but if you have something in common, it may lead somewhere. First impressions are sometimes reversed!

Try to keep in mind that if she's genuinely interested in you, she will give you a second chance, or a third or fourth. As you get to know her, she might grow to like you more and more. If you're still unsure about how you're date is going, just be honest: tell her that you're a bit nervous because you really like her. She'll be swept off her feet!

**IF SHE'S GENUINELY INTERESTED IN YOU, SHE WILL GIVE YOU A SECOND CHANCE, OR A THIRD OR FOURTH.**

# WHEN YOU'RE A TEENAGER, DATES CAN SEEM LIKE A BIG DEAL.

## How embarrassing

One of the worst things that can happen on a date is that you embarrass yourself, or your date humiliates herself, and then both of you are too awkward to continue. It might be something silly, like spilling a drink on yourself, or something a bit worse, like the girl unexpectedly getting her period. These things happen, and you have to be ready. The best way to deal with embarrassment is to laugh it off—but if your date embarrasses herself, take cues from her. If she is not laughing, DO NOT laugh at her. She might think that you're making fun of her, and she will probably end the date and not talk to you again. Another example is if you trip over, just get up calmly, make a joke about how you're totally uncoordinated, and keep going. If your date falls over, help her up, ask if she's okay, then say nothing for a while. If she still looks embarrassed, try a little joke or tell her about one time that you fell over or made a fool of yourself.

## Try to have fun

When you're a teenager, dates can seem like a big deal. But you have to remember that you're not going to be getting married and

THE GREAT THING ABOUT DATING
WHEN YOU'RE A TEENAGER IS THAT
IT GIVES YOU VALUABLE EXPERIENCE
FOR WHEN YOU'RE OLDER.

# IF YOU DO SCREW UP A DATE OR IT TURNS OUT THAT SHE DOESN'T REALLY LIKE YOU, IT'S NOT THE END OF THE WORLD.

having babies for many years (hopefully!) so just take it easy. There's no need to rush or be too serious about the whole thing. Try not to appear too laid back or she might think you're not having a good time or enjoying her company. But while you're still a kid, try to have fun. When people remember their favourite date, it's not usually the most perfect or most romantic one. It's the one where you both joked, laughed, made fun of the movie you saw, missed the bus and had to walk home. Things don't always turn out how you planned, so just go with the flow and try to make sure you both have a good time.

## Puppy love or true love?

People are always saying that there are more fish in the sea and it sounds like a total cliché. But if you do screw up a date or it turns out that she doesn't really like you, it's not the end of the world. When adults tell you it's just puppy love and you'll get over the heartbreak, they're not trying to be mean! They say it because they've been through it when they were young. It's no less important—in fact, when you're young, romance can seem extremely vital. A lot of this is because you don't have any prior

## A GOOD THING TO KEEP IN MIND WHEN ON A DATE IS THAT, FOR TEENAGERS, 'TRUE LOVE' IS PRETTY RARE.

experience, so every date seems like the most important moment of your life! Perhaps you don't feel like this: you might be more laid back, and think that it's not that bad if a date doesn't work out. But lots of teenagers feel very strongly about their early encounters with the opposite sex.

You might not care if a date doesn't go very well, but maybe the girl you went out with is completely crushed! So you have to be sympathetic if your date is a bit upset afterwards. It can be very confusing trying to work out your feelings, especially if they are very strong, or if a girl feels very strongly about you. A good thing to keep in mind when on a date is that for teenagers, 'true love' is pretty rare: in other words, most people that you date when you're a teen won't end up being your lifelong partner. Some couples that get together when they're teenagers do stay together, but a lot of them don't. Puppy love in itself is a beautiful thing. And the great thing about dating when you're a teenager is that it gives you valuable experience for when you're older.

## SOME PRACTICAL TIPS FOR DATING

» Be confident—be yourself and don't act like a phony.
» Don't brag about yourself—it's insulting to some girls
(and boys for that matter).
» Ask questions—but don't go crazy with them.
» Dress decently, not like a slob—make sure your clothes
fit your personality.
» Keep yourself clean at all times—girls love guys
who put a lot of effort into their appearance.
» Find some conversation starters—
and listen to what she has to say.
» If she laughs at everything you say—
then she definitely likes you.
» Don't be afraid to make eye contact—
make sure you smile. Don't stare.

## WARNINGS

» Don't use pick-up lines—they could be just
plain stupid and offensive.

» Don't stare at any part of her body—girls can tell
when you are not paying attention.

» Don't grope her inappropriately—that may blow your chance.

» If you're going to invite her to hang with your friends—
don't ignore her and just talk with your friends.

» Don't cling onto her the entire time—let her have her freedom.

» When trying to hold her hand—if she doesn't hold
yours back, let go.

# Where to go?

The big question is where to go on a date. If you live in the city, there are lots of choices, but maybe too many choices. If you live in the country there might be a lot less to choose from so you don't have a choice at all. 'You have to take her somewhere, you can't just see her at school and say hi,' Will (13) said. The best thing for a date is to make it in a public place—like the movies or a cafe—because if things don't go too well, you can always end the date early. Once you've had a few dates in public places and you feel comfortable with each other, you can invite her to your place, or go to hers. Try not to go on a first date to someone's house. If you don't feel comfortable you might feel a bit trapped. It gets awkward if you want to excuse yourself. And climbing out of the bathroom window is definitely not going to leave you on good terms.

*The movies:* Lots of people go on first dates to the movies. Maybe you both like obscure foreign films, or maybe you both just want to go to the latest comedy. Keep in mind that everyone has different taste in films—some people love blood and gore, others might feel a bit sick at the thought of seeing a horror film.

It's good to be a gentleman and let her choose the film, but don't become a doormat. If she wants to go see a tear-jerking chick flick, and you know you'll be bored out of your brain the whole time, you should let her know nicely. Comedy is a nice, safe bet for most people. Just remember that you're more interested in her than the film. If you're not, then maybe you should reconsider your date!

*A cafe or restaurant:* A lot of guys imagine taking their date to a romantic restaurant, but not every guy can afford that. You don't have to pay for both of you—it's fair enough to expect that each of you will pay for your own food. But it's great to be able to take a girl to lunch or dinner, and it will make her feel special. Even though you might not be able to afford French cuisine, you don't need to end up at McDonald's. There are plenty of cheap restaurants and cafes that serve real food. If you don't know any local cheap eats, do some checking. A lot of places will have menus in the window so you can look at meal choices and prices.

## 'YOU HAVE TO TAKE HER SOMEWHERE, YOU CAN'T JUST SEE HER AT SCHOOL AND SAY HI.'

# 'YOU CAN'T DO SOMETHING THAT THE GIRL DOESN'T LIKE TO DO, YOU CAN'T FORCE THEM.'

Otherwise you can just go inside and ask a waiter or waitress what their price range is. If you suss it out before the date, you'll know where you're going when you to meet her rather than wandering around looking for somewhere suitable. Otherwise, you can ask your date where her favourite cafe or restaurant is, and whether she'd like to go there if it's a reasonably priced one.

*Ice skating and bowling rinks:* It's fun to do something different on your date, so why not go ice skating or bowling? These things don't cost too much and they usually sell food on the side. You can get a bit competitive with each other on the playing field and have some fun at the same time. The good thing about going ice skating or bowling is that you have something to do on the date and then it won't get awkward when one of you runs out of things to say. There're also plenty of opportunities to chat while you play.

There are lots of other things you can do on a date, such as seeing a band; going to a festival; trying rock climbing, horse riding or fishing; walking on the beach or in the bush; going shopping; hanging out at a youth centre; or browsing the markets. Try to find something you'll both like, and make it a date!

## To kiss or not to kiss?

You'll probably be thinking about this when you're on a date—should I kiss her or not? Charlie (13) told me, 'You can't do something that the girl doesn't like to do, you can't force them.' It's important to recognise this and know what you want and be able to work out what she wants. Maybe you can't wait to lock lips, or maybe you're a bit shy. One thing's certain: kissing can be very awkward. If you go in at the wrong moment, it could be a disaster! You need to be able to read the signs and get your timing just right. Here are some answers to the questions that might be going through your head.

### KISSING CAN BE VERY AWKWARD.

*Why does she keep touching my hand?* If she keeps brushing her hand against yours, then she probably wants you to hold her hand. Handholding is a gesture of intimacy. Basically, she's saying 'I like you and want to touch you'. It doesn't mean 'Kiss me right now', but it does mean kissing might be around the corner.

*I've got my arm around her . . . what next?* So you're sitting there watching a movie, and you've gotten cosy enough to put your arm around her. Your heart's racing and you're trying to work out what she wants you to do next. She might be a bit freaked out too. This can get very uncomfortable, especially if you have a million thoughts flying around in your head. Here's a tip: whisper something in her ear and see if she turns to face you. It's all about eye contact. If she gives you a long look in the eyes, she may want you to kiss her. If she blushes and looks away, you should wait a while longer.

*I gave her a kiss on the cheek and she ignored me, what's wrong?* Maybe she doesn't feel comfortable about kissing you. A peck on the cheek is a good way to test the waters. It can be a bit freaky going in for the full mouth kiss, so try little kisses on her hand, cheek or neck first.

A positive response would include some of the following: letting you kiss her, giving you a little kiss back, extended eye contact, hugging, touching your face or hair, putting her hand on your knee or side.

A negative response would include very different body language:

**ANOTHER GOOD IDEA IS TO GO OUT IN GROUPS.**

pulling away from you, looking away instead of at you, folding her arms, going stiff instead of relaxed, looking around to see if people are watching you, or pretending that nothing happened.

Pay close attention to how she reacts. If you're brave, ask her how she feels. If you feel a bit embarrassed after your advance, just let it pass.

*She keeps kissing me—why is it making me feel weird?* If your date decides to take the initiative and make a move on you, you might discover that you're not actually that into it. Perhaps you thought she was cute, but then discovered that kissing her just didn't feel right. It's better to speak up than go through a whole date saying nothing. Plus, by saying nothing you'll give her the wrong impression. Use a kind tone of voice to tell her that you're not feeling comfortable, and you'd like to slow down. Just

say the sort of thing you'd like a girl to say to you if the situation was reversed. Remember that you could easily embarrass her, so just try to be nice.

*Our date was great—why didn't we kiss?* Don't worry! You don't have to kiss on a first date. Sometimes it's better to build up a bit of trust between you. If you continue to go on dates and you don't kiss, then maybe you guys are better as friends. Or maybe you're both too shy to make a move. Keep in mind that the 'right moment' might never come. It doesn't have to be perfect when you kiss the first time. Usually it's a bit sloppy and wet and you might laugh about it afterwards. Also, don't be afraid to ask. If it's been ages and it feels right, just say, 'I really want to kiss you.' She might have just been waiting for you to ask!

# EVEN IF YOU ASK A GIRL ON A DATE AND SHE SAYS 'NO', YOU CAN STILL BE FRIENDS.

## No date and still friends

Asking someone on a date can be a bit traumatic, especially if she says 'no'. But it's not something you don't recover from. The best thing is to just play it cool. When you ask her on a date, do it casually. Don't buy her flowers or chocolate—that might make you feel silly if she says 'no'. A good way to ask a girl out is to ask her to go with you to a specific thing; for example, a movie that's showing on the weekend. If she says 'yes', you can go along and see how it goes. Doing something alone together doesn't necessarily mean you're on a date. It may very well be you and your mate, who happens to be a girl, seeing a movie together. This might turn into something more while you're out, or if you do it again some other time. Remember, when you ask a girl out it doesn't have to be a date. This takes the pressure off a little bit when you're asking her.

Another good idea is to go out in groups—some of your friends and some of hers. You can get to know her within the safety of your group of friends. But if you do want to ask her out on a real date, be prepared for her to say 'no'. Don't be too confident. And if she says 'no', don't pursue it. You can say something like, 'Maybe next time' or 'That's okay, see you round', but you need to respect a girl's right to say 'no'. If you're really game, you could tell her that you're a bit disappointed because you like her and thought it would be fun to go on a date. She might think about this and decide to take you up on your offer. But it's up to her to pursue this. If you keep asking her out all the time, it's harassment.

Even if you ask a girl on a date and she says 'no', you can still be friends. Maybe for a week you'll feel a bit stupid and want to avoid her, but it's good to keep being her friend after that, especially if you were friends before you asked her out. People's feelings change over time, and in a year or so she might decide to go on a date with you. Or maybe you'll go on dates with other people and find a boyfriend or girlfriend. One of the most important lessons in life is coming to understand what kind of relationships you have with people. It's not always clear who is a friend and who is a potential girlfriend. This sort of knowledge comes with time and experience.

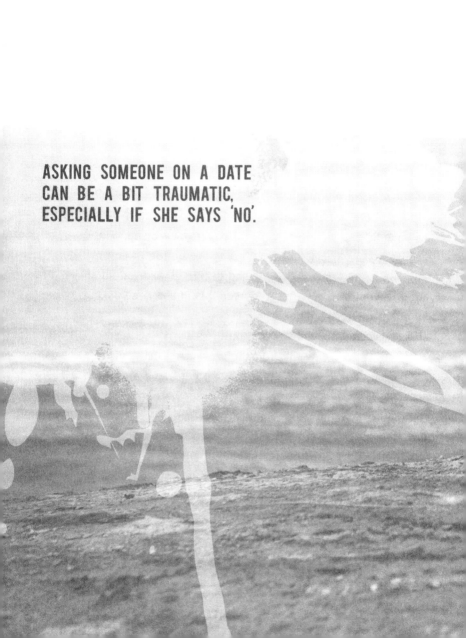

ASKING SOMEONE ON A DATE
CAN BE A BIT TRAUMATIC,
ESPECIALLY IF SHE SAYS 'NO'.

# 6 SCHOOL DANCES, FORMALS AND SOCIALS— A SURVIVAL GUIDE

School dances may get some people excited; for others they strike fear in their hearts. A number of people see dances as more of a girl thing, but dances, formals and socials are meant to be a chance for boys and girls to socialise outside of class. The problem is, how do you survive the gruelling experience? When a school dance is announced, the first thing people start talking about is who's going with whom. You might see this as a great opportunity to ask that girl you think is really hot to be your date. Or you might be groaning and wanting to hide under a rock whenever someone asks who you're going with. This survival guide should provide you with a few pointers so you won't feel so helpless.

## Asking her to the dance

If you really want to ask a girl to go with you to the dance, formal or social, then you should go for it. If you don't ask, you don't get. Don't fear rejection—it's part of life and if you can accept that you'll probably win some respect among your mates. There are certain ways you can go about asking her that will save you embarrassment if she's not interested. One good way to ask a girl to the dance is to do it quietly. Ask her when she's alone. If you

**#1 RULE**

Don't be a bitter loser. If she rejects you, just play it cool. There's no need to slag her off afterwards just because she didn't want to go with you.

can't get her when she's alone, ask for her phone number so you can call her later on. Plan what you're going to say to her. Don't just blurt out 'Youwannagodancewithme?'; start off by saying you think she's really interesting/smart/funny/cute/hot/pretty and that you'd really like to go to the dance with her. If she's not interested say, 'Thanks, maybe another time.' She might have just said 'no' because she didn't know what to say, so if you're friendly and polite after getting rejected, she might think of you again later.

## When you don't want to ask a girl

People can get pretty crazy about the whole 'who are you taking' thing. If it gets a bit much for you, don't stress. Most people don't take dates to school dances. There's a lot of talk that goes on in the lead up to the dance, but in reality there will be quite a few people who genuinely want to go together, a bunch of others that are only going together because their friends are doing it, and then another large group of people that don't want to go with anyone in particular. The people who have dates might try and make you feel like you couldn't get a date—school dances can sometimes turn into a bit of a popularity contest. Don't stress. You'll probably have the last laugh when you go to the dance and realise that most boys are standing on one side of the room and most girls are standing on the other side of the room.

## IF YOU DON'T ASK, YOU DON'T GET.

### #2 RULE

Do what feels best—if you want to go alone, be proud and remember that a lot of people will be going alone too. At least you don't have to coordinate your outfit with someone else's.

### #3 RULE

You probably won't miss much by not going to the dance, but if you're staying at home to avoid socialising, just remember that you have to see these people five days a week, and learning to interact with them is pretty important.

KEEP YOUR MIND OPEN. THOUGH SCHOOL DANCES MAY SOMETIMES SEEM BORING OR STUPID. THEY CAN ALSO BE FUN.

## You don't want to go—that's okay

School dances aren't for everyone. If you feel like you get enough socialising done at school, or if you have friends outside of school that you'd rather spend time with, you don't have to go. If you know someone else who's not going, you could do something else with them instead, like going to a movie, or hanging out at home listening to music you actually like and eating something other than sausage rolls. Keep your mind open. Though school dances may sometimes seem boring or stupid, they can also be fun.

## To dance or not to dance?

Most people look kind of funny when they dance, unless you're a dancer—in which case you should rip it up on the dance floor, no problems. If you're worried about how you're going to look if you dance, try practising in a mirror or asking a girl for some tips (now that's a good opening line if ever there was one). If there's no way you'd be caught dead shaking your 'thang' at the school dance, then don't worry about it. But keep this in mind: a lot of girls like to dance, and they like having boys to dance with. If you're willing

A LOT OF GIRLS LIKE
TO DANCE, AND THEY
LIKE HAVING BOYS
TO DANCE WITH.

**#4 RULE**

Try to have fun while dancing—it will make the whole experience more enjoyable.

to have a bit of fun at the risk of looking a bit stupid, you might find that you're pretty popular with the ladies.

## When your date won't talk to you

Sometimes boys go to all the trouble of asking a girl to the dance, and when you get there, you can't get her away from her group of friends. Laura (14) explains, 'When you go out with your friends and agree to meet him there, you mainly stay with your friends. But if you get a lift with him, you might stay with him the whole night and then just talk to your friends on the side.' Sarah (17) comments that 'most girls would only feel comfortable talking to other girls', adding that it 'depended on the person: The group can be a security blanket for a girl. Everyone is insecure and she could feel more comfortable with her friends.' If you really want to spend some time with her, ask her to dance or just go over and talk to her. If she's already said she'll go with you, chances are she's probably interested in getting to know you. School dances might not be the best time to talk to a girl. You might want to use the dance as a chance to ask her to do something else, like going shopping or hanging out with you on the weekend. If she really doesn't want to talk to you, let her keep her distance.

Remember that people can change their minds, and she may have realised that she's not interested or she may just be too shy to talk.

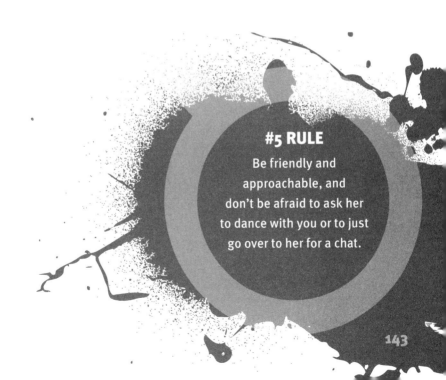

### #5 RULE

Be friendly and approachable, and don't be afraid to ask her to dance with you or to just go over to her for a chat.

## Is she my girlfriend now?

If you think the dance went pretty well and now you'd like to see more of this girl, how do you ask her? It's a good idea to get her phone number or email while you're at the dance, if you don't already have it. That way you can get in contact with her afterwards to talk about how it went. Ask her if she had fun, and what she enjoyed most of all. If she sounds friendly and interested in talking to you, tell her that you had a really great time with her and that you'd like to see her outside of class some other time. If she sounds interested, ask her where she'd like to go. Make sure you have an idea of somewhere you'd like to go so you can suggest it if she doesn't know anywhere. If she tells you the dance was boring, or she sounds like she doesn't want to chat, just give her some space. You can always try talking to her again at school.

### #6 RULE

If you really like her, pluck up the courage to call her afterwards! You don't want to leave it too long and make her think you're not interested.

IT'S A GOOD IDEA TO GET HER PHONE NUMBER OR EMAIL WHILE YOU'RE AT THE DANCE.

# 7 MENDING BROKEN WINGS

Making friends with a girl might seem pretty hard, but keeping them as friends can sometimes seem even harder. One minute they think you're the funniest guy on earth, and then they storm off a few minutes later! You might want to blame it on PMS, but girls sometimes have pretty good reasons for getting pissed off. Boys might push a joke too far, or just say something that's offensive without even realising. Girls can ask some confusing questions, like 'Do you think my bum looks big in this?' Boys can be a bit clueless sometimes, and might answer that honestly.

Girls often get upset when boys don't know when to use white lies. Usually this ends up with the girl going off in a huff and not speaking to you for a few days. Getting the cold shoulder can be tough, especially if you feel bad for hurting her feelings. You might think that it'll all be okay soon enough, and she'll get over it and start speaking to you again. But this isn't really the best way to solve the problem. If you break a bone, and leave it to heal by itself, it might get better, but it won't be as good as it was before. If you break a bone and set it properly, it will have a much better chance of working like it used to. It's kind of the same with girls. If you leave her alone, she'll probably get sick of hating you after a

MENDING BROKEN WINGS

few days (hate takes a lot of energy) but she'll always remember the time you upset her, and how you didn't really make up with her. Maybe this means she'll like you less, or maybe she'll look for other male friends. Or maybe when you need her, she won't feel like helping you. Some people are good at holding grudges, and other people think it's a waste of time. But people will always remember when you hurt them, whether they hold it against you or not!

## Was it something I said?

'But what did I do?'; 'I didn't do anything wrong!'; 'She's just crazy!': sound familiar? It's a common problem faced by boys your age. Sure, girls might be unreasonable sometimes, but at other times boys just can't see why their words or actions would upset a girl. Mood swings are pretty common in all teenagers, but boys and girls sometimes use different emotions to express themselves. Boys can get angry, irritable and silent, whereas girls may get teary, emotional and snappy. In order to work out what went wrong, you have to try and understand what she's feeling, and think about what you might have said or done to make her upset. Jack (14) told me how to make up with a girl: 'Say sorry, ask "What do you want me to do to make it up for you?" If she's my girlfriend, give her a kiss on the cheek.' Here's a step-by-step guide to patching things up:

**Step 1: Backtrack.** Remember back to what happened before she got upset. What were you talking about? What was going on while you were talking? Try writing a list of everything you remember happening in the lead up to your fight. Things that happened a few days or week before might be relevant, or it might just be the things that happened a few minutes before. Writing it down will help you remember, and seeing it on the page might help you make some links and sort out why you guys started fighting.

**Step 2: Think about your tone of voice.** Sometimes you think that what you said wasn't really that bad. But you have to remember girls don't just listen to your words. It's not what you say, it's how you say it. If you were in a bad mood and you said something to her that was supposed to be nice, but it came out sounding sarcastic, she might be offended because she thought you were

MENDING BROKEN WINGS

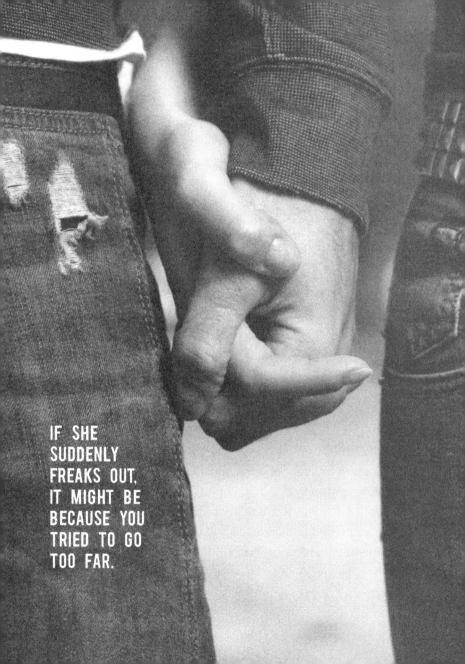

IF SHE
SUDDENLY
FREAKS OUT,
IT MIGHT BE
BECAUSE YOU
TRIED TO GO
TOO FAR.

# IF SHE DOESN'T SEEM LIKE SHE'S HAVING TOO MUCH FUN, THEN BACK OFF.

being rude. Or maybe you were feeling bored, so you sounded like you didn't care. When you say things, you have to sound like you mean it, or she won't be very impressed.

*Step 3: Think about the words you used.* Other times, it's just bad word choice. Maybe you were trying to sound really sincere, but you just said the wrong thing. It's a mistake most people make now and then, so don't beat yourself up over it. But girls can get really pissed off if you say the wrong thing, especially if they didn't realise that your intention was to be nice, not mean. If a girl asks you what you think of her hair, and you tell her it looks like a bird's nest, she's not going to like you. Think of your words like a toolbox—you have to choose the right tool for the job, or you'll mess up. Before you answer a question, think about the best way to respond. Instead of saying, 'Your hair looks like a bird's nest', say, 'I prefer your hair when it's nice and sleek'. If you respond in the positive rather than the negative, she's less likely to get annoyed at you.

*Step 4: Did you cross her boundaries?* If you were getting close to a girl, you might have thought that you could go a little bit further.

# YOU NEED TO MAN UP AND JUST ASK HER, 'WHY ARE YOU UPSET WITH ME?'

But girls have their own boundaries that they don't always want you to cross. Sure, she may have been getting comfortable with you, but if she suddenly freaks out, it might be because you tried to go too far. The best way to prevent this is to ask her how she's feeling. If she doesn't seem like she's having too much fun, then back off. It will only make both of you feel bad if you pressure her into doing more than she wants to. If you think you may have crossed her boundaries, then you need to find out from her, or she probably won't want to see you again.

*Step 5: Talk to her.* This is the best way to sort things out. There's no point sitting around wondering what went wrong. You need to man up and just ask her, 'Why are you upset with me?' If you've been thinking about it for a while and you have an idea about why she got mad at you, you might want to start the conversation like this: 'Was it because I said . . . ?' Sometimes if a girl is still upset, she will try and pretend that nothing happened, or she won't answer your questions honestly. That's when you need to jump in with an apology: 'I'm sorry if what I said upset you. I didn't mean to make you feel unhappy.' If you think she's still angry,

# SOMETIMES A SMALL GIFT IS A GOOD WAY TO GET THE BALL ROLLING AGAIN.

it's a good idea to apologise, because that might make her more willing to talk to you. She'll see that you're sorry for whatever you did, and that you want to talk to her about it and fix things between you. Giving an honest apology is the best way to start the conversation.

**Step 6: Give a small gift.** We all know that actions speak louder than words, so sometimes a small gift is a good way to get the ball rolling again. Don't go all out with roses and chocolate—you might just embarrass her. The best type of gift to give in this situation is something handmade, or a card. Maybe you can make her a CD of some music she likes, or pick a flower on the way to see her. Something little and inexpensive is a nice gesture, and she will appreciate your thoughtfulness.

**Step 7: Remember that it might not have anything to do with you.** Girls and boys have a lot going on in their heads when they're teenagers. Things can be pretty confusing, and sometimes you'll feel depressed or irritable for no reason at all. If you've had a good think about what happened, and you've talked to her and

ONE THING THAT GIRLS REALLY HATE IS WHEN
GUYS TRY TOO HARD TO IMPRESS THEM.

she's told you it had nothing to do with you, she might be telling the truth. Maybe she was already upset about something else, like a fight with her best friend, or family problems. If she tells you it's not your fault, ask her if she wants to talk about what's upsetting her. She might not want to, but at least you're showing that you care and are willing to listen. If she gets upset at you all the time for no reason, there might be some bigger problem she's dealing with, like an eating disorder or depression. Try to be a good friend by making her feel comfortable enough to tell you what's going on. If it's serious, you might need to encourage her to get help. But just remember, adolescence is a pretty tough thing to go through, and boys and girls need to look after each other, not fight with each other all the time.

## Trust in yourself and try less to impress

One thing that girls really hate is when guys try too hard to impress them. I know it can be difficult to work out—when is it too much? when is it not enough? Guys are constantly thinking about how to get a girl's attention, but when you try too hard, you can run into a lot of problems.

*When funny is not funny.* Have you ever tried to make a joke, and it just didn't work? Maybe they didn't get it, or maybe what you said wasn't really that funny. Here's a tip: try not to tell offensive jokes to people who'll be offended easily. Sexist, racist or homophobic jokes don't really have a place anywhere, but if you're going to tell them, at least tell them to a mate or someone whose reaction you can guess. Trying to impress a girl by saying something 'funny' about fat chicks isn't going to go down well. Be careful when you're trying to impress a girl by being funny—try to get to know her sense of humour first, so you know what kind of jokes she'll like.

## NOT EVERY GIRL WANTS A TOUGH GUY.

*Risky business: Is it worth it?* Sometimes guys try to impress girls by being tough and doing dangerous things. If you don't get hurt, then you must be pretty good. If you do get hurt, you take it like a man. Can't lose, right? The thing is, girls aren't really interested in dangerous games. You're probably only going to prove that you're immature. Stuff like this might impress your

## THE MORE YOU LET THE REAL YOU OUT, THE MORE GIRLS WILL BE INTERESTED IN YOU.

mates, but girls are probably more interested in the things you do that won't kill you. Even if a girl is impressed, do you really want to risk hurting yourself just to catch a girl's eye? There are plenty of other ways to impress girls, in far less risky circumstances.

*Mr Tough Guy.* You might think that strutting around and flexing your muscles will impress a girl, and you might be right! But picking on others so it looks like you're tough is not on. There's no point trying to be a bully just to get a girl. You'll probably find yourself making more enemies than friends. Some girls like big muscly guys—maybe it makes them feel safe, or maybe they just like the beefcake look, but if your arms are more like string beans, don't worry. Girls go for different things in guys, and some like boys with a more modest physique. Don't stress out about going to the gym and working on your pecs—not every girl wants a tough guy.

*When bad hair days are every day.* Making sure you look good used to be what girls worried about, not guys. But these days, guys are under more pressure to look their best. Just think of metrosexuals—those guys in pink shirts with sculpted moustaches and styled hair. Metrosexuals are out to impress the ladies, but at what price? Cologne isn't cheap, and it takes a long

LOOKS CERTAINLY PLAY A PART IN ATTRACTING A GIRL, BUT IT'S DEFINITELY NOT THE MOST IMPORTANT THING.

time to do your hair just right. If you're trying too hard in the looks department, you might end up looking a bit vain, or a bit shallow. Looks certainly play a part in attracting a girl, but it's definitely not the most important thing, as any girl will tell you. Most girls are looking for a guy who will treat them nicely, talk to them and want to have some fun. Your hair won't be able to do the talking once you've got a girl interested in you.

There's a middle ground between trying too hard to impress a girl, and being so laid back it seems like you don't even care. This middle ground is called being yourself. It may seem a little strange, but the more you let the real you out, the more girls will be interested in you. Being yourself shows that you're honest, confident, and don't need to be someone else to impress girls. If you think the real you isn't very exciting, then maybe you need to do some more exciting things—learn how to play guitar, do some volunteer work, get involved in extra-curricular things at school. Don't try to be impressive by pretending or exaggerating—just be yourself.

# 8 SAME-SEX ATTRACTED TEENS

Gay, lesbian, bisexual and transgender teenagers have friendships and relationships just like heterosexual teenagers. Some things will be exactly the same: wondering if someone's interested in you, thinking about who you like, and getting the guts to ask someone out. But there are things that gay guys go through that are different to what straight guys experience. Because being gay is part of your sexuality, it affects your relationships and how you interact with other people. Straight guys might find it daunting to ask out the girl they like, but imagine what it's like for gay guys! Not only are you thinking about the other person, you're also thinking about yourself, and wondering who you are.

It's pretty hard trying to work out whether you're gay. It's likely that most of the people you know are straight. A lot of the gay guys presented by the media are stereotypes. And while there may be plenty of boys in your school, how many feel the same way that you do? Gay teens often feel isolated and worry about not being 'normal', but try to keep in mind that there are plenty of well-adjusted, happy people in the world who also happen to be gay. The problem is sometimes just a matter of finding the right people to connect with. Many same-sex attracted teens

# HAVING A CRUSH ON A BOY WHOSE SEXUALITY YOU ARE UNSURE OF CAN BE A SCARY BUT EXCITING EXPERIENCE.

join groups or find online forums to find other young gay people. There's even a Gay and Lesbian Counselling Service in case you're feeling alone or sad.

It's not always easy being gay. Even if you've accepted your sexuality, you might be experiencing mixed feelings or confusion from friends, family members or people at school. All of this can make things very complicated for you, especially if all you want to do is have a relationship with someone. How do you know when to go for it? Many gay guys feel isolated because they don't know anyone else who is experiencing similar feelings to them. Everywhere you look, you see straight people!

When you find someone that you think might also be gay, it can be a wonderful thing. But how do you know for sure if they are gay? Dan, who's now 22, talked to me about when he was a teenager: 'I never approached anyone without knowing before if they were gay. I wouldn't have taken the chance.' Going to guys who have already come out can be one way of ensuring you have a safety net but as Dan says, 'I always knew they were gay even before thinking anything. I had this gut feeling that they were gay.' But this might limit your options. For some guys, having a crush on a boy whose sexuality you are unsure of can be a scary but exciting experience. It's a good idea to get to know him as a friend first. Also, getting to know his friends may provide you with the opportunity to ask questions about him. However, there can be problems associated with having gay male friends. As Dan said, 'All the gay boys I knew when I was younger were not friends but possible boyfriend material that ended up becoming boyfriend material . . . I am still kind of sceptical about having gay friends.' Lots of straight people approach people of the opposite sex that they are attracted to under the guise of friendship, so don't feel weird about saying you want to be friends when really you want to get in his pants. A friendship that ends up becoming sexual or a full-on relationship is still a valid connection to make.

As you start looking for gay guys there may be certain things you start to notice. Some gay guys play up to the stereotype to make their gay identity more visible. But everyone is different and there is no one particular way that gay guys look, act or talk. Gays come in all shapes and sizes, all nationalities, all religions and all ways of life. However, Elliott (20) believes there may be something that you can use to tell if a guy is gay: 'There is

'I NEVER APPROACHED ANYONE WITHOUT KNOWING BEFORE IF THEY WERE GAY. I WOULDN'T HAVE TAKEN THE CHANCE.'

# 'THERE IS A CERTAIN WAY A BOY WHO'S INTO BOYS WILL SMILE AT YOU.'

a certain way a boy who's into boys will smile at you.' It isn't a failsafe method, but the 'gaydar' that some people talk about can be fairly effective. 'Gaydar' means the ability to recognise other gays instinctively or by picking up on very slight indications, such as a particular smile, or a particular way of sitting or handling something. The problem is that in high school, many guys are unsure of their sexuality. You might even be unsure yourself. When people are unsure of their sexuality, they may try to hide it. This can make it very difficult for sussing out who is potential boyfriend material. As you get older and more comfortable and open about your sexuality, you will probably find it easier to meet and connect with gay guys.

## Where are all the gay guys?

You might feel like you're the only guy in your year, or even the whole school, who is having these feelings about guys. This can lead to isolation, which is also linked to depression and suicide. People don't always understand or tolerate homosexuality, and teenagers are already prone to depression and feelings of alienation. This can be a very difficult time for you. It's important

## THE PROBLEM IS THAT IN HIGH SCHOOL, MANY GUYS ARE UNSURE OF THEIR SEXUALITY.

to make sure you feel connected. But how do you get connected to the gay community when you don't even know anyone who's gay? The internet has made it much easier to find and talk to other gays. Dan (22) says 'Now, with the internet, you can ask anyone for advice. There are forums everywhere. Just Google your question and there's bound to be something.' The internet can be a good way to find gay guys your age in your local area, but it can also be a great place to make online friends that you can go to for advice or just to chat. It's also useful for finding resources that are designed to support gay guys. If you don't have access to the internet, or don't feel safe using it at home or in an internet cafe, you can still get in touch with services in your area as there are support helplines you can call that support gay and lesbian teens. Some places run weekly programs for gay teens, sort of like a youth group, where you can meet other gay guys and get access to important things like free condoms and info on sexual health. As you get older you may want to go to gay bars, saunas or men's gyms. These places are often used by gay guys as places to pick up, but can also be a safe place to socialise with other gays. As a teenager you may feel like you're the only one, but

COMING OUT IS A DIFFICULT DECISION.

there might be guys sitting right next to you who are struggling with the same feelings. Just remember that there are people who want to provide support for you, who already understand how tough it can be growing up gay, and who are more than happy to put you in contact with other gays.

## Coming out or keeping quiet?

One way to make yourself visible to other gays is to be open about your own sexuality. Coming out is a difficult decision—in some ways, guys who come out can feel more free to be themselves and less burdened by the secrecy and shame of trying to hide their sexuality. But being openly gay means having to deal with homophobia. However, many people suffer homophobia even when they are not openly gay, or not gay at all! Some guys feel more freedom by keeping their sexuality a secret. That way, they can move between the straight world and the gay world as they please. Josh (18) says relationships are different for gay teens because 'you have to be more secretive about it. You can't be open about it. Which really sucks sometimes but then again, secrets make it more fun.' Other guys just want to wait until they

## SOME GAY GUYS JUST WANT TO HAVE SEX, BUT OTHERS ARE LOOKING FOR A MORE SERIOUS OR LONG-TERM THING.

know for sure that they are gay before they tell people about it. One thing's certain: it helps to have information on coming out and to listen to other people's coming out stories before you decide to do it.

## Relationship or not?

Deciding whether or not you want a relationship is tricky for any teenager. However, things can be a bit different when it's two boys, rather than a boy and a girl. Elliott (20) says, 'Boys who do boys tend not to form relationships. Or if they do it tends to start out as sex the night they meet and become more after that.' Some gay guys just want to have sex, but others are looking for a more serious or long-term thing. The experiences people have when they are teenagers help them decide what they want when they're older; so don't worry too much if you're not sure what you want now. Even older people (straight and gay) can be very confused about what they want.

Making mistakes in relationships is one way to learn what you do and don't want. Dan (22) says one mistake he made when he was younger was 'accepting things I would never usually accept,

## MAKING MISTAKES IN RELATIONSHIPS IS ONE WAY TO LEARN WHAT YOU DO AND DON'T WANT.

like dating someone that defends Celine Dion while bitching about Bjork'. Going out with a guy just because he is gay is something a lot of gay teens do. As you get to know more gay guys and have more options you will probably start to connect more with guys who share your interests or values. Advice that Dan would give to young gay guys is: 'Don't get attached to someone too easily. Gays tend to do that at first, because they don't know many gays. So as soon as they meet one, they go berserk. But then again, there's nothing really wrong with that. You've got to learn from your mistakes.' When you meet someone who you think is really special, and you know he likes and is attracted to you, don't be afraid to pursue it. Remember that it's your life and you're allowed to be happy, so if you want a relationship, go for it. If you need to discuss any of your concerns, worries or fears, remember there's always a counselling service or a helpline.

## REMEMBER THAT IT'S YOUR LIFE AND YOU'RE ALLOWED TO BE HAPPY, SO IF YOU WANT A RELATIONSHIP, GO FOR IT.

# CONCLUSION

Talking to girls can be challenging for a guy. Although you can get away with not saying much most of the time, at some point you'll find yourself in a situation where you will have to talk to girls.

When you learn how to comfortably talk to girls, you will notice many rewards. Girls respond to boys who seem comfortable and confident. They will like talking to you and will want to repeat the experience. And when you learn to talk to girls naturally and confidently, you can then apply your new social skills to everything you do throughout your life.

How do you get used to talking to girls? By practising. Although it might be awkward at first, keep at it! If you embarrass yourself when talking to girls, it's tempting to give up. But everybody has bad experiences; learn from them, bust through your comfort zone and enjoy the ride!

## HOW DO YOU GET USED TO TALKING TO GIRLS? BY PRACTISING.

RESOURCES

## Suggested books

*100 Things a Boy Needs to Know* by Bill Zimmerman
    (Free Spirit Books, 2005)
*Boys' Stuff* by Wayne Martino and Maria Pallota-Chiarolli
    (Allen & Unwin, 2001)
*From Boys to Men: All About Adolescence and You* by Michael Gurian
    (Price Stern Sloan, 1999)
*Puberty Boy* by Geoff Price (Allen & Unwin, 2005)
*Puberty Girl* by Shushann Mousessian (Allen & Unwin, 2004)
*The Puberty Book* by Wendy Darvill and Kelsey Powell (Hodder, 1995)
*The 'S' Word: A Boys' Guide to Sex, Puberty and Growing Up*
    by James Roy (University of Queensland Press, 2006)

## Websites you can look up

Just key in 'PUBERTY IN BOYS' on Google and you will find many;
for example:

Puberty in Boys (www.avert.org/puberty-boys.htm)
Boys and Puberty (kidshealth.org)

## Helplines you can call

Kids Helpline 1800 55 1800 (Australia)
Lifeline 13 11 14 (Australia)
Gay and Lesbian Counselling Services and Youthlines:
ACT 02 6247 2726
QLD 07 3252 2997; rural areas, toll free 1800 184 257
SA 08 8422 8400; rural areas, toll free 1800 182 233
NSW 02 8594 9596; rural areas, toll free 1800 184 527
VIC 03 9827 8544; rural areas, toll free 1800 184 527
WA 08 9486 9855
TAS 1800 184 527

These services are anonymous, and calls to an 1800 number do not appear on a phone bill. You can chat to someone about your feelings and they can answer many of your questions. They can also tell you about support groups and social functions.

Pick up a gay and lesbian newspaper. Every state has gay and lesbian newspapers that will tell you about what's on and how to access support and social groups. There are also national magazines available, some of which you can subscribe to.

# INDEX

First published in 2011

Allen & Unwin
Sydney, Melbourne, Auckland, London

83 Alexander Street
Crows Nest NSW 2065
Australia
Phone:    (61 2) 8425 0100
Fax:      (61 2) 9906 2218
Email:    info@allenandunwin.com
Web:      www.allenandunwin.com

Cataloguing-in-Publication details are available
from the National Library of Australia
www.trove.nla.gov.au

ISBN 978 1 74237 194 8

Cover and internal design by Seymour Designs
Internal photography by iStockphoto
Printed in Australia by McPherson's Printing Group

10 9 8 7 6 5 4 3 2 1